Relationships

IN THE MILLENNIUM:

⤜ A WORKBOOK FOR LOVERS ⤛

Relationships
IN THE MILLENNIUM:
❧ A WORKBOOK FOR LOVERS ❧

DR. JOAN D. ATWOOD

iUniverse®

Relationships in the Millennium: A Workbook for Lovers

iUniverse books may be ordered through booksellers or by contacting:

iUniverse
1663 Liberty Drive
Bloomington, IN 47403
www.iuniverse.com
1-800-Authors (1-800-288-4677)

Because of the dynamic nature of the Internet, any web addresses or links contained in this book may have changed since publication and may no longer be valid. The views expressed in this work are solely those of the author and do not necessarily reflect the views of the publisher, and the publisher hereby disclaims any responsibility for them.

Any people depicted in stock imagery provided by Thinkstock are models, and such images are being used for illustrative purposes only.
Certain stock imagery © Thinkstock.

ISBN: 978-1-4917-9291-9 (sc)
ISBN: 978-1-4917-9343-5 (e)

Print information available on the last page.

iUniverse rev. date: 07/11/2016

A primary need is to love and be loved.
This book is dedicated to those who have risked this journey

TABLE OF CONTENTS

1

INTRODUCTION

It is rather ironic that while we have schools for driving, cooking, hairdressing, and a host of other crafts, skills, and occupations, there is no school for one of the most important aspects of our lives— relationships. Not only is there no school or course of instruction in relationships, but also there is no preparation for the decision to marry. So that while it is a decision that we enter into for supposedly the rest of our lives, it is a decision that we make without any training. And in this day and age, with the extended life span, we are talking about living with the same person for fifty or sixty years!

So, while the decision to marry is one of the most important emotional, social, and legal commitments we make in our life, it is often entered into not only not knowing our own personal self and relationship needs but those of our intended marriage partner as well. As a result, the not knowing creates a situation that is ripe for fantasies, illusions, and unrealistic expectations of our partners and ourselves. Based on these fantasies and illusions, we often have unrealistic expectations about how our relationship will be and in the beginning tend to overestimate and idealize the interests, goals, and values that we share. In this way, the stage is thereby set for shattering disappointments when reality sets in.

The complicated processes involved in making the decision to get married or enter into a serious, committed, relationship, is further muddled by the idea that the decision to make a commitment should be a spontaneous, natural process. The idea that we cannot and should not prepare for marriage because it will and should happen spontaneously is further reinforced by the movies and TV. We are very carefully taught that we will "know" instantly when the "right" one appears. In a small, informal survey that we conducted, 100% of the people interviewed answered, "I would just know," in response to the question, "How will you know when you've found the person you want to marry?" When we asked married persons the same question, they answered in the same way— "I just knew." This is a very curious phenomenon, this "knowing" and we are in the process of gathering information about the nature of "knowing."

In any case, assuming that we "know" when the "right one" comes along, it is difficult to appreciate, in the glow of romance and sexual arousal and stimulation, how the realities of day-to-day living will change our long term feelings toward our partner. As many of us know, the joys and excitement of a new relationship can give way to the demanding routines of everyday life and often partners feel that the love and romance has gone out of the marriage.

It is our belief that while many of us walk down the aisle with enthusiasm and a sense of certainty, there are others of us who say that deep within them they knew that they were making a mistake or that they felt they really didn't love the other person. Some say that they realized that they were not acting wisely but that they were afraid of hurting their partner, or disappointing the expectations of their family and friends.

To these individuals, we wish to extend our support and encouragement to listen to, to develop further, and to trust their intuition and introspective processes regarding their relationship decisions, and to have the courage of their convictions. To the others who were surer of their decision, we wish to help them understand how the processes of intimacy will develop and what vulnerabilities and defenses will be activated as intimacy deepens. For both, we have provided information and experiential exercises that will hopefully assist them in this process. Often, couples feel that no matter what happens, whatever problems they have, that the power of their love will conquer these difficulties. To these individuals, we wish to provide information and education around these issues of love and mate selection and the psychological factors involved in these processes.

We are faced with the fact that in our culture many marriages are failing and many exist in a state of chronic unhappiness. Take a moment to close your eyes and think about your friends, your relatives, and people you know who are married. Think of their marriages. Are they happy? Are their marriages something you would want for yourself? It is probably true that you didn't come up with a very high percentage of marriages that you would define as "happy." At least 50% of marriages in the United States end in divorce. America has the highest divorce rate in the world. In addition, there are an additional 300,000 marriages that are terminated as a result of annulment, legal separation, or desertion. And we know from simple observation that the remaining marriages are not in a state of chronic bliss.

This book, then, represents an effort to assist those who are contemplating a long-term relationship or marriage and also to aid those who are already married. The focus of this book is to help people to be more knowledgeable about the factors associated with a greater chance for personal and relationship happiness and to help raise your awareness, the consciousness of individuals. In the following chapters, we explore the nature of love, intimacy, commitment, responsibility, and mature relating. We will endeavor to help whoever is reading this book to openly and honestly evaluate their relationship so as to be appreciative of possible signs and symptoms of impending problems, which can then be more constructively addressed. In addition, we will point out common patterns of relating in couples with their accompanying emotional difficulties and offer guidelines for possible growth. Although many of the vignettes describe heterosexual couples, the statements, insights, and suggestions apply to all types of couple relationships, whether they be heterosexual, homosexual, bisexual, transgender, etc. Throughout the book, we have provided experiential exercises, which will engage the reader in a process of a more conscious relationship.

While committed relationships can be fraught with many burdens, responsibilities, pressures, conflicting needs, and unfulfilled expectations, they can also provide a deep sense of meaningfulness, companionship, sharing, and intimacy. It is the author's belief, as we will explore in later chapters, that love is the most fundamental energy in the universe, and that it's fullest expression is intimately intertwined with the empathy and understanding which the more aware relating process offers. It is also the most essential ingredient of a sense of harmony and fulfillment which most of us strive for. The educational material, the case histories, and the exercises presented throughout the book are the culminations of many years of assisting clients, friends, students, and ourselves through relationship struggles.

Throughout the book are quotes from Brian, age 8, a young boy who was asked his opinion on these topics. In many ways, his wisdom is enlightening. So, we offer this book as a beginning, a start, in helping persons to explore their own capacities for love as they can be released in the relationship process.

EXERCISE: The Little Wise Person

This first exercise is one of our favorites and we would like to share it with you as one that you may take with you not only throughout your reading of this book, but also as one you can call upon to aid and assist you throughout your life.

Imagine that you are walking down a long winding path. There are trees and flowers everywhere. The day is bright and you feel cheerful. You hear the leaves crunching under your feet as you make your way down the lovely winding path. The sun, beating on your face, feels warm and comforting. As you walk around a bend, you notice a person at the far end of the trail. The person is wearing a white flowing robe tucked at the waist with a belt. The wind is gently blowing through the person's hair.

As you approach the person, you notice the person is holding a red rose. You know deep in your heart that this is very, very wise person.

Using your imagination, ask the person three questions which are very important to you.

1. _____

_____

2. _____

_____

3. _____

_____

After each question, wait for the wise person to answer. Write down the little wise person's answer as carefully as possible.

1. _____

_____

2. _____

_____

3. _____

_____

Think very carefully about the questions you asked the little wise person and the answers the little wise person gave you and what they mean to you. Write down any additional thoughts.

_____

_____

_____

_____

_____

The Little Wise Person is really you. This person lives deep inside of you and guides you and helps you through life as you embark on new stages of life and new adventures. This little person will be with you forever and may be called upon at any time. This person is all kind, all knowing, and if you trust this person fully will always lead you in directions that are good for you. This person accepts you, protects you and teaches you. This person is your intuition.

2   LOVE: THE SOCIAL DEFINITION

"Because we're in love" is the reason most Americans give for wanting to get married. Love is the element, which is regarded as giving meaning to human relationships. There is no way that the concept of "relationship" can be explored without first examining the whole idea of "Love." The definition of Love covers everything from God's love of human beings to pistachio ice cream.

There is probably no term more widely used and abused in the English language than love. We love our parents and our dogs, our brothers and sisters, and our cars, our sweethearts and our new dress, our country and flag, malomars and oreo cookies. We love animate and inanimate objects, vegetables and fruit, attitudes and behavior. Love is the overwhelming topic of concern for songwriters, novelists, journalists, and teenagers.

We get married because we love our future partner and we get divorced perhaps because we love our children and do not want to see them get hurt. Some Americans kill other people because they love their country and freedom whereas some other people abandon their country because they love it and their freedom.

Love is a complex perplexing force that all of us experience in many different ways. It varies in intensity from time to time and dependent on the object can be consistent and inconsistent at the same time.

So when we speak about love, who knows what we're speaking of? On the one hand, love means a strong sexual attraction to another but on the other hand it means intense affection. It can mean concern, emotional attachment to a treasured object, but it can also mean passion. We can love our children, our parents, our pets and our careers but we can also love our mates, partners or another's partner. We can love someone for sentimental reasons. And we love them differently. We can fall in love, be in love, love someone and fall out of love.

WHAT IS THE HISTORICAL EVOLUTION OF LOVE?

Love as we know it has not always been around. There are probably four phases through which the concept or idea of love has evolved historically. The first occurred in the fifth century B.C. in the Greek culture of Plato and the first century A.D. in the Roman culture of Ovid.

Plato, writing about upper class Athenians, felt that love would inspire virtue. He divided love into two types: common and heavenly. For Plato, a common love could either be homosexual or heterosexual in focus and it concerned itself with physical satisfaction. A higher type of love, heavenly love, was primarily spiritual in nature and existed between two men.

Ovid's conception of love was sensual and heterosexual in focus, what Plato called common love. Ovid did not view love as a force that existed inside marriage. Rather, it was the experience that a man had with a married woman in an adulterous affair. Ovid offers suggestions that might be made by a lover to the married woman he loves as to how she can project her love to him in the presence of her husband when all three are at a party. He also offers advice to the Roman woman who wants to be attractive. In essence, Ovid saw love as a game to be played in the social arenas of Roman Life.

The second phase in the evolution of love occurred in the twelfth century in the courts of Europe. This kind of love is known as courtly love. It refers to an abstract and distant love, as man would have for a woman other than his wife. The sexual drive was sublimated and the expression of courtly love took the form of unselfish loyalty and devotion of the knight to the lady. The cultural significance of this concept, courtly love, is that the idealization of the female initiated her social elevation and that it introduced voluntary fidelity, restraint, and the magnanimous gentleness of the male consciously into the relation between the sexes, qualities that were not considered essential or even possible in a marriage based on the semi patriarchal concept of the middle ages.

Most historians date the American ideal of romantic love back to the Middle Ages to this phenomenon of courtly love. In medieval times, marriage was based primarily on social and economic factors— love had nothing to do with it. For love, the courtiers of the European society turned to partners outside of marriage. This courtly love apparently did not involve sex. Rather, the man idealized the woman and was supposed to perform courageous and virtuous acts on her behalf, but she was considered too pure to be a sex object.

The third phase through which love evolved began in the fourteenth century and continued into the seventeenth and eighteenth centuries. During this time the courtly love ideology filtered down out of the castles into the villages, and cities rather slowly at best. The court society of the seventeenth and eighteenth centuries redefined the distant and nonsexual orientation of courtly love to include sexual favor outside of marriage. By the seventeenth century it became acceptable for love to be an experience encountered by a man and a woman who were engaged to be married.

Finally in the nineteenth century, the concept of love moved into the fourth phase when the Romantic Movement in art and literature with its emphasis on the primacy of feeling and of the tragic elements of human existence further intensified the Western ideal of romantic love as the be-all and end-all of life.

Romantic, or courtly, love in its classical form, was asexual. It emphasized loyalty, service, and devotion to the ideals of feminine beauty, and masculine chivalry and has had enormous influence on the manners and morals of European society from its inception in the eleventh century as a literary concept right up to the present. The concept of romantic love persisted in much the same form well into the 1960s, as embodied in nursery tales, song lyrics, comic strips, movies, and novels. Tarzan of the Apes and Flash Gordon can be considered direct lineal descendants of Sir Lancelot.

Since the mid 1960s, though, the popular emphasis on romantic love has shifted somewhat, toward an acceptance of sexuality as a concomitant of the romantic ideal; and this version is reflected in current mass media.

The social setting of Europe, in which the concept of romantic love developed, clearly separated romance from the institution of marriage (and still does to some extent). Marriage was arranged by families and was based on practical considerations unrelated to whatever personal attraction a young man and woman might or might not feel toward each other. Marriage was not an institution to provide for the fulfillment of personal desires but a sober relation that provided for societal and economic needs and for the establishment and maintenance of the family.

Marriage and sex relations were contained within an official relationship, whereas romantic love ... remained outside of marriage on an individual basis. Marriage was the public and responsible one. Marriage was permanent and stable, a means of conserving property, and rearing children ... romantic love lasted only so long as the personal preference for each other was fervid (see also Cavan, 1969)."

Contemporary American society demands that romantic love be a primary basis for marriage; and once married a person is usually expected to derive his/her personal and romantic satisfaction form within the framework of his/her marriage. If extra couple romantic involvement does occur, the cultural expectation is that it must either be discontinued or institutionalized by divorce and remarriage.

Contemporary romantic love is characterized by three elements:

- The traditional asexual idealism of service, chivalry, devotion, and exaltation of feminine beauty and virtue,
- The acceptance of sexuality as an extension (or concomitant) of this ideal, and,
- The emphasis on marriage (or at least a fairly permanent relationship) as the ultimate expression of this ideal.

People have stated that they believe the values of romantic love seem to contradict those of marriage. The emphasis in romance is on freedom; the emphasis in marriage is on responsibility. Values in romantic love are personal; in marriage they are familial. Romance is private, tumultuous, idiosyncratic, and characterized by an intensity of experience and heightened awareness; marriage is public, stabilized, routine, and often mundane.

The love ideology has evolved to a point where it is considered both an essential prerequisite to marriage and the cementing force that holds a married couple together. But love, like most other cultural phenomena has come under criticism. The romanticists see love as the salve that miraculously cures all pains; the cynics see pain and disorganization as a result of relying on love, an emotional experience, instead of on rational and systematic thought. Goode, a family sociologist, notes that the introduction of a love ideology in some cultures is very disruptive. He refers to societies in which marriage is essentially an arrangement in between families tending to support the existing social stratification system. To allow love as a basis for mate selection is antithetical to the prevailing patterns of interaction and exchange in such societies.

Despite many contradictory characteristics between romance and marriage, romantic love is not necessarily opposed to married love. Romantic love may not only continue after marriage but conceivably may even be enhanced by it, although such an occurrence is unfortunately rare. We believe that if a person identifies with his/her mate as a real person, rather than as a projection of his/her own idealized needs, couple satisfaction can deepen the romantic love of dating and courting. But if identification is not founded on reality, disillusion will inevitably occur because the close and constant everyday contact characteristic of marriage forces an acknowledgment of the reality of the person rather than the idealized vision.

WHAT ARE SOME DEFINITIONS OF LOVE?

"Love is feeling free to go out into the world and do your own thing and then coming back home to your partner for hugs." Brian, age 8.

"Love: Well, love is, uhm, Love is when you <u>really</u> like someone. You <u>really</u> have a crush on them. It's when you <u>really</u> like each other. Like you really like each other. A Lot! I mean A LOT! And that's love. When it's extremely, you love a person. Your feelings really expand over to each other." Brian.

What is love? Can you define it? Conceptualize it? Sort it out? How do you know when you're in it? Out of it? What are its essential components? Is the love you feel for your sweetheart, friend, parent, child the same emotion? How are these loves the same? How are they different? Let's limit ourselves to romantic love— the kind usually claimed by two people, the kind that each will probably use to justify a commitment to marriage and "living happily after."

The word love is extremely difficult to define, for although it is widely used, it is used in so many different ways it can mean almost anything. For the same reason we cannot simply assume that everyone intuitively knows what is meant by love. We must attempt to capture it in as accurate and useful a definition as possible. For love is a very real and extremely important element in all primary relations and especially in the paired relations of dating and marriage; and if we are to understand the formation and interactions of these relations, we must understand the concept of love.

In order to reach a shared definition, we will begin with an examination of some of the commonly accepted characteristics of love:

- The ability to feel and express love is apparently learned through cultural conditioning, although the need to experience demonstrations of love is innate and essential to survival in infancy and to well being in adulthood.

- Love is not an all-or-nothing phenomenon. It can exist in many different degrees. It may simply be the ultimate of like or it may be the type of passionate, totally absorbing attachment celebrated in literature and the arts. It should be noted that there is some evidence that "liking" and "loving" are not necessarily two degrees of the same emotion, but may be two different emotions. In researching the characteristics of "liking" and "loving", Rubin found that with his sample, and using his testing instrument, the correlation between "liking" and "loving" was only moderate. Rubin defined "liking" chiefly in terms of respect, and "loving" chiefly in terms of attachment or caring.
- Love may have many different forms. The love object may be concrete (a person, animal, or thing) or abstract (liberty, justice, adventure, art, mankind, God), and the motivations for love are as diverse as human personality.
- People believe that love has objective reality. It is not a myth. The experience of love is among the most powerful experiences of man or a woman. Love has at its basis some unknown force or energy that is real, although it has not yet been isolated and identified by science. Researcher Sorokin suggests that the energy of love is a strong creative, recreative, and therapeutic power that generates a response of energy in the recipient and thus creates a chain reaction of love energy exchanges between the two persons in a love relation.

For our operational definition of love we will subsume all of what we can consider its various aspects and conclude that love is a vital and profound emotion that is experienced as a result of a significant need satisfaction. In other words, a person in love derives a deep, compelling, persistent, and positive emotional satisfaction from the love object— a satisfaction that may be the most significant and highly motivating experience known to human beings.

Some Classic Definitions Of Love Include:

Love is Security

When the satisfaction or the security of another person becomes as significant to one as is one's own security, and then the state of love exists (Harry Stack Sullivan).

Love is Energizing

Love is an active power in man; a power which breaks through walls which separate man from his fellow men ... In love the paradox occurs that two beings become one yet remain two (Eric Fromm).

Love is Growthful

Love is the passionate and abiding desire on the part of two or more people to produce together the conditions under which each can be and spontaneously express his real self; to produce together an intellectual soil and an emotional climate in which each can flourish, far superior to what either could achieve alone.

Love is Sacrifice

Love is that intense feeling of two people for each other which involves bodily, emotional, and intellectual identification; which is of such a nature as to cause each willingly to forego his personality demands and aspirations in favor of the other; which gains its satisfaction through creating a personal and social identity in those involved.

Love is Lust

Love is an irresistible desire to be irresistibly desired (Robert Frost).

Thus, love is significant for personal, couple, and societal reasons and as we have seen it also occurs under predictable social and psychological conditions. This implies that while our society sets the stage for love feelings to develop, individuals need to have certain characteristics, which will enable them to experience these love feelings.

EXERCISE: Researching Your Future Mate

Imagine that a woman looking for a husband wants to use objective, rational criteria for making her final love choice. After all, she investigates every other major purchase she makes— so why not research one of the most important investments she'll ever make. In her investigation, she will try to control for emotional influences with the exception of possibly some feeling of physical attraction, which would have some significance for her future sexual contentment. So, our hypothetical woman meets a physically attractive man and must decide if he is the man to marry. After making sure (she has a checklist) that he is of approximately the same age as she is, the same socio-economic class as she is, the same ethnic, educational, and religious background, she will put him through a number of assessments. First, she could turn him over to a board of psychologists and psychiatrists. They could probe his psychological makeup, and measure his intelligence, motivation, aspirations, and the overall strengths and weaknesses of his personality. His potential as a husband and a father and provider, his mental health and stability might also be assessed.

Second, she could turn him over to a group of biologists and medical experts. His family background could be thoroughly examined to determine possible genetic skeletons in his family closet and possible positive genetic contributions he might make to their children. The state of his physical health and some estimate of possible life expectancy might also be established. A third test would subject him to a variety of new social experiences, with the results used to analyze his ability to adapt and adjust adequately. As a final test, he might be followed day and night for at least six months by a competent private detective agency and a final report sent to her.

Sounds ridiculous? Perhaps, but as we stated in the introduction, when we buy a car, a stereo or most anything else for that matter, we research the product, examine it, ask others about it, and sometimes try it out before we buy it. Yet, when we choose a partner, we tend to leave the selection process to our hearts or to chance. What we are hoping in writing this book is that we have raised enough considerations for you to ponder when deciding on a potential mate. The exercises provided throughout the book are intended to help you in this process.

Some Questions That Will Help You Evaluate Love:

• Are you comfortable and at ease with your partner? Are you able to be yourself without feeling nervous or uncomfortable?

_____

_____

_____

• When you are with your partner, are you more inclined to live up to your best conception of yourself and your abilities?

_____

_____

• Are you conscious of a continuing stable bond between the two of you, even when you are not feeling feelings of love?

_____

_____

• Does this person really matter to you, regardless of emotion or lack of emotion at the moment?

_____

_____

• Would you love your partner just as much even if s/he were sick instead of well, or even if his or her physical appearance should be marred or disfigured?

_____

_____

- Is s/he physically attractive to you, so that you have no inclination to apologize or feel defensive about his or her physical characteristics?

  _____

  _____

- Are you proud to be seen together?

  _____

  _____

- How well do you agree on the things worth working for in life?

  _____

  _____

- Can you talk over points of disagreement and reach an understanding?

  _____

  _____

- Have you known each other long enough and well enough so that you have discovered your inevitable points of disagreement?

  _____

  _____

- Do your disagreements result in a better understanding of each other or do they remain unresolved and you tend then to argue about the same issues over and over?

  _____

  _____

When disagreements result in tabling and blocking off the issue, or in the same one's always giving in. This is a danger signal.

- Do you have confidence in your partner's judgment? Do you respect his or her general intelligence?

_____

_____

_____

- Do you confide in this person freely, with complete confidence that what you say will be understood, judged kindly, and never carelessly divulged no matter what the temptation?

_____

_____

- Are you happy and satisfied with the way your partner shows affection for you?

_____

_____

- As you look toward the future as realistically as you can, do you feel that the two of you have in your relationship the elements that will enable you to cooperate and love each other for your continuing union?

_____

_____

_____

_____

3   WHAT ARE THE DIFFERENT TYPES OF LOVE?

"Well, there's two types of love. There's the love that you love someone and there's the other love. Okay, it's the same thing as "S." It's the same thing as sex. It's the same thing." Brian.

If any of the many attempts to define love during the past 3,000 years have anything in common, it is their diversity. However, the traditional assumption is that the many forms that love may take in a relationship are all derived from various combinations of the four components of altruistic love, companionate love, sexual love, and romantic love.

Altruistic Love

> *I love taking care of Jay. I love doing his wash and running errands for him. I like that he knows all the little things are taken care of. This way he doesn't have to bother with them or worry about them. Sometimes he's just like a little boy. He gets so cute, especially when he's looking for something he can't find, or if he's supposed to leave for work and can't remember where he put his brief case. You would never know he's a successful attorney by watching how he is when he's at home.*

Altruistic love implies an emphasis in the relation on the well being of the love object. If providing nurture brings the provider an intrinsic satisfaction, this emotion (especially when sustained and enhanced) may be defined as altruistic love. Providing for another may bring a person more satisfaction than providing for his/her own well-being. This is so because needs exist in a hierarchy, and the need to provide nurture for another person may take precedence over the need to provide nurture for one's welfare.

Companionate Love

> *Jon and I have a comfortable relationship. We like doing a lot of the same things and share many similar interests. We spend our days working at our respective jobs and then come home, have dinner, and relax quietly by the TV. Sometimes we read instead of watching TV and on Saturday nights we usually go to a movie. We never argue. Whenever we have a disagreement, we talk about it until it's solved. When we were first married, we used to have sex more frequently, maybe once a week. But now that we've been married for a while, it's less— sometimes we almost forget to have sex. Some people would say our lives are boring but we enjoy the quiet life. We've worked out our lives in a very easy manner and that is how we like it.*

"Liking" and "loving" are somewhat different. "Liking" is certainly more characteristic of more relationships more of the time than is the deep, "caring for" involvement of love. That is, a couple committed to one another in a love relationship do not always share a mystical plane of mutual ecstasy most of the time, and certainly married couples normally live at the more modest emotional levels of mutual respect, affection, and companionship more often than they do at the exalted heights celebrated by poets, dramatists, and songwriters. This is not to say that the idealistic cultural expectations for ecstatic love are never fulfilled; such dreams may be not only fulfilled but also surpassed. But the companionate component of love, although the least dramatic, is probably the most commonly and frequently experienced (and thus, in this sense, is the most important) aspect of married love, despite mass media emphasis on romance and sexuality.

Sexual Love

> *Lou and I have an intense relationship. We relate to each other in a "heavy" way. We never talk about things like the weather or world politics. Whenever we see each other, we spend a lot of time just looking at each other and talking about important issues and feelings in our lives. I know everything about him and he knows everything about me. We can never be together for an extended period of time without touching one another. Once we start, this usually leads to making love. Sometimes we'll plan a quiet evening at home with a nice dinner, candles, and some wine. Usually before dinner is over, we're in the bedroom. It just seems like we can't keep our hands off each other.*
>
> *Occasionally, we'll have arguments that get pretty heated. We start off shouting at each other and before long we're in the bedroom again. Sometimes the issues don't get resolved and we argue about the same things over and over again.*

Love is frequently associated with the experience of sex, or with sexual attraction and fulfillment. This is not to say that love always involves sex; obviously it does not. It is equally obvious that sex does not always involve love. However, some measure of emotional involvement- or sexual love- usually occurs in all but the most cursory sexual relations.

Sexual love, or the emotion which a person experiences when the love object is also the sex object, is characterized by:

- Strong feelings of tenderness, admiration, and esthetic appreciation.
- A strong need for tactile and, usually, genital contact.

Sexual participation then becomes an extension of the intimacy and communication of the relationship. When persons experience sexuality and orgasm together, and this is accompanied with feelings of love and affection, the consequent experience of satisfaction and depth of involvement with the other is almost mystical in its intensity- although the capacity for sensory and emotional involvement varies among individuals just as does the capacity for love (and for that matter, all other capacities).

One aspect of sexual love that is especially important in contemporary American marriages is its function in the couple interaction as a conformation of the love relation and of the mate as a significant other. Like such nonsexual couple activities as preparing and eating a meal, conversing, or providing solace, sex can be a love offering; or it can be a strategic move in a couple power struggle, which is the conflict over dominance in a couple relation. Or it can help to regulate closeness and distance in the relationship. But because sex is unique among couple activities in its inherent motivational strength and its deep emotional effect, a nonreciprocal or resentful or unloving sexual relation is usually much more destructive to the happiness and stability of a marriage than divisive behavior in nonsexual areas. Further, the societal expectation of sexual loyalty to a mate places even greater responsibility on sex as a component of couple success.

Thus, when sex functions in a marriage as a chief confirmation of love, it is sometimes enough to keep a couple happy, even if there is no significant congruence in other important areas of their marriage. But without sexual love, a marriage will be successful only if sex is not significant in the perception of both individuals and if both of them receive important mutual confirmation from each other in significant nonsexual areas- for example, companionship or extreme altruism, and dependency.

It is important to point out that this emphasis of sexual love in marriage is largely a trait of the Western, and particularly the American, society. In other societies, where marriages are arranged, and in simple societies, where the woman's role is chiefly homemaking and childbearing, sexual love plays a much smaller role in marriage.

Inasmuch as the identification of sex and love is so prevalent in our society, it must be emphasized that sex and love are not the same, although they share many important characteristics. Both demonstrate physical, physiological, motivational, emotional aspects (like the reproductive aspect of sex is physical and physiological, but its pleasure-giving aspect is emotional); yet it is possible to experience sex without love, love without sex, or sex and love together.

Romantic Love

> *Wally is everything to me— my friend, my lover, and my confidante. He's intelligent, good looking, supportive, nurturing, and lots of fun. I would rather be with him than with anyone else. It's just so nice to be with him. We always have a nice time when we're together. When I'm not with him, all I do is think about him. I'll remember back to the last time I was with him— the last time he kissed me or the fun we had the time we went to the beach. Sometimes at work I'll find myself daydreaming about him instead of doing my work.*
>
> *When we make love, it's so wonderful; it feels like we're sooo together. I think we'll probably get engaged on Valentine's Day. I know he'll make such a wonderful husband. We get along so well; we never even argue. I just love him so much.*

Human beings appear to have potential for romantic love, but this potential is only realized under favorable social and cultural conditions. For example, in Tahiti, Samoa, and the Marquesas, romantic love is completely unknown. When one anthropologist asked the Tahitians to describe their passionate feelings, they were incredulous. They had never heard of anyone feeling like that. Was such a person, they wondered, mad?

And yet, although romantic love is found in most industrialized countries, it appears to have reached its zenith in the United States. Our society not only places great value on romantic love, but also provides a climate highly favorable for its development. Our society expects us to fall in love, and most of us do. By their late teens, more than 90 percent of American men and women have fallen in love— often more than once. And for most of us, love is a prerequisite for marriage.

The concept of romantic love and the importance it plays in Western society could actually be a factor influencing the high divorce rate. If romantic love is "supposed" to be present in a couple relationship, as soon as the couple falls into a comfortable, day-to-day routine, they may feel disappointed and frightened, perhaps thinking that the love has gone out of their marriage. It is important to note that the intense romantic and sexual feelings that couples refer to as love cannot be maintained over long periods of time. The business of daily living must go on. It would be impossible to function in a responsible and competent manner if one's energies were so directed to and absorbed by the loved one.

What Is Romantic Love?

Psychologist Rubin developed a questionnaire to measure the nature, depth, and intensity of romantic love. He has found three basic components that he considers to be essential to romantic love:

- Attachment defined as a need for the physical presence and emotional support of the other person.
- Caring defined as a feeling of concern and responsibility for the other person.
- Intimacy defined as a close bond manifested in part by confidential communications.

Researchers Walster and Walster have similarly defined romantic love. They prefer to use the term passionate love which they say is the wildly emotional state associated with strong physiological arousal, a confusion of feelings, intense absorption with and longing for the loved one, and a strong desire for fulfillment through this person. This definition puts greater emphasis on the intense emotional state of romantic love—a state characterized by a profusion of feelings including tenderness and sexual desire, ecstasy and pain, altruism and selfishness, vulnerability and jealousy.

Dorothy Tennov calls this intense passionate state "limerence." In her studies of people who have experienced limerence, she found the following characteristics of this type of love:

- Intrusive thinking about the loved one crowds all other interests and concerns into the background.

- The person experiences a deep and acute longing for the loved one to return these feelings.

- The person experiences mood swings dependent on the actions- or an interpretation of the actions- of the loved one. S/he experiences feelings of buoyancy or "walking on air" when love is returned and of "heartache" when the loved one's sentiments are uncertain.

- The person is shy and clumsy in the presence of the loved one, crippled by fear of rejection.

- The person is unable to have such intense feelings for more than one person at a time.

- The person emphasizes the loved one's positive points and overlooks or minimizes faults.

- The person has a strong sexual attraction to the loved one.

Tennov found that the moment of falling in love is often an intense one, ignited by a biochemical spark and involving a magical, intoxicating feeling of being in love. Because of the magical feeling that many experience upon falling in love, it is not surprising that up until recent times romantic love was thought to result from the intervention of supernatural powers, such as a dart from Cupid's arrow, a love potion, or a sorcerer's spell.

A final important component of love, especially in dating and mating, is that of romance or the idealization of the love object. Romantic love falls within the generic definition of love, yet possesses characteristics that seem to differentiate it from companionate love, altruistic love, and sexual love. Romantic love is a very complex and subtle aspect of the emotion, and observers are by no means in agreement in defining the dynamics of romantic love, or even in accepting its validity as an operational element in mate selection or marriage.

Some observers have suggested that romantic love occurs as a result of blocking the drive for sexual expression. From this point of view, since sex is usually readily available in marriage and a married person cannot therefore be presumed to be sexually frustrated, it would be impossible for him/her to be romantically in love. Critics of this view consider such a hypothesis much too ingenuous. Their own explanation is that romantic attraction can occur as an end in itself, independent of sexual needs or frustrations. Anthropologist Malinowski found that strongly individualized passionate and enduring romantic attractions occur among the Trobriand Islanders whose society openly accepts sexual activity.

The prevailing opinion in our society regarding romantic love is that it may occur, and persist, and even deepen in a relationship characterized by sexual satisfaction rather than by sexual frustration. This view accepts two separate and distinct needs, sexual and romantic, but hypothesizes that these two needs are closely related and ultimately interdependent in love affairs or in marriage. The sex need is chiefly physical, the romantic need chiefly emotional; but both needs may be satisfied by the same person, who is then both the sex object and the romantic love object. Thus, the gratification resulting from sex will also be an emotional satisfaction, which will reinforce feelings of love and the need for romantic involvement. This kind of sexual contact will produce an intense intimacy and immediacy of communication and will strengthen a couple's mutual commitment to each other.

As with all love, romantic love apparently originates in the nursery, in the comfort and support and fondling that the child receives from his/her mother or care-taking person. Thus, the chief focus of affectional life in infancy is the mother or caretaker, and affectional life is paramount in the infant's awareness. As the infant grows to be a child, and as the child matures, other interests crowd in upon his attention: the need to develop mastery and manipulative skills, to acquire esteem, and to actualize his/her potentialities. Affective life does not necessarily diminish, but a variety of other concerns also become important. With adolescence, however, affective needs once again become central. The drive to satisfy them is generally no more self-consciously sexual than it was during infancy; rather, the adolescent's preoccupation with love may be almost entirely asexual and romantic. But from the middle teens to the mid-twenties, this preoccupation shifts to a fusion of sex and romance. And from the mid-twenties on, the preoccupation is probably chiefly sexual.

In mature romantic love, persons enter a state in which the supreme motivating factor in their life is their devotion to another person, and of equal or greater importance, their personal satisfaction from this devotion and the response to it. Not only does each person see the other as an idealized version of his/her sexual need but also each in turn tries to fulfill the ideal of the other. In dating and all other romantic interactions, the principal role each person plays is to fulfill the romantic expectations of the other (as well as his/her own), in order that as a pair both people will conform to the romantic pattern as they have learned it. They wish to be alone with each other because privacy and secrecy make identification easy, and the two build up a feeling of oneness and of separateness from the world. They create and exist in a little world of their own, furnished with their shared memories. This kind of intense emotional response and great preoccupation and involvement with each other may occur with little or no physical contact; merely talking, holding hands, or lightly kissing may be experienced as deeply satisfying. Also, the person in love with someone who is not physically available may forego sex with another who is available in order to remain faithful to the romantic ideal.

Romantic love places the highest value on personal characteristics. A person is more discriminating in his/her choice of romantic love object than in the choice of a sex object, because the sex object need not have the many specialized requirements of the romantic love object. Romantic love is focused on the nature of the goal object; sexual attraction is concentrated essentially on the strength of the drive for sexual release. An initial attraction may be sexual and then develop into romantic love, or the relation may be at first a romantic one, which later comes to include sexual love. In either case, in our contemporary society, the expected outcome of this attraction would be marriage. Just as there is a range of feeling from liking to loving and from romanticism to realism, there are different types of loving.

Love In America:

The American tradition of romantic love has developed over the centuries out of the courtly ideal. It may be summarized as follows:

- **Love at first sight.** Love involves an immediate recognition of the one and only right person, even if the love is not returned.
- **Love is blind.** The lover idealizes his/her beloved and is oblivious to any faults or limitations.
- **Love conquers all.** The love must be so strong that it can overcome all obstacles, from parental objections to adverse economic conditions.
- **Love is both agony and ecstasy.** The person in love alternates from joy and despair, depending on how the romance is faring.
- **Love is passionate.** Love is characterized by an intense desire for sexual union with the beloved.

Most social scientists define types of loving. These types are ideal constructs. Rarely is anyone a pure type. Rather, persons have varying degrees of each quality.

Eros (Romantic) Love

I know what kind of person I'm going to marry. He'll be tall; about six feet tall- I like tall men. He'll have a medium build. I don't like skinny men; I always feel fat when I'm with a skinny man. He'll have light color hair, preferably blond. And he must have blue eyes— blue eyes look like the ocean. He'll have light skin but the kind that tans well. I love a tan body in the summer. And, of course, he'll have nice teeth, straight, even, and very white. Also, I hope he wears Drakar cologne. The smell of Drakar just turns me on. Oh, and he'll have some hair on his chest, but not too much— just enough for me to run my fingers through. I'll know immediately when I meet him that he's going to be the person I spend the rest of my life with.

Some people say that I'm too picky — that I'll never find exactly what I'm looking for. But I will, I just have to keep looking. There's always one "right" person for everyone and I'll find my "right person" sooner or later. I just have to be patient.

The Eros style of loving is similar to romantic love. Eros individuals seek a lover who is the perfection of physical beauty. They hold on to an ideal image in their thoughts and try to find the person in real life. The image involves the details of the lover's skin, eyes, hair, body proportions, and even fragrance. When the person is spotted, and they "know" immediately that this is "the" person, there is the feeling of having known that person for a long time. Individuals who fall in love often or who have been in love several times are likely to view love through a romantic set of lenses.

This type of love is characterized by an immediate powerful attraction at first meeting, accompanied by such physiological reactions as increased pulse rate, shortness of breadth, trembling, and such sensations as a tight band across the chest or a fluttering in the stomach. Looking into the other's eyes can cause a sensation of approaching shock, so that sustained eye contact becomes virtually impossible.

Erotic lovers usually experience a chemical or gut reaction on first meeting each other and go to bed soon afterwards. More than any other kind of love, Eros is characterized by an active and imaginative interest in sexual fulfillment. Eros people typically press for an early sexual relation, and usually become lovers shortly after meeting. Nothing is more deadly to Eros than a lack of enthusiasm or a puritanical approach to sex. If the Eros person is attracted to someone who is not freely erotic, his joy and the elation will probably disintegrate. This is the first test of whether the affair will continue, since erotic love demands that the partner live up to the lover's concept of bodily perfection. However, the erotic relationship also involves psychological intimacy. Each wants to know everything about the other, to become part of him or her. They like to wear matching "T" shirts, identical bracelets, matching colors, order the same foods when dining out etc.

Erotic love is the most transient of the various styles of loving. Because the real must match the ideal in terms of physical beauty and psychological fit, the erotic lover is often disappointed. Although erotic lovers may eventually settle for less, they never forget the compromise and rarely lose hope of realizing the dream.

The Eros style of loving seems to be more characteristic of men than of women. As research has shown, men appear to be more romantic in their conception of love than women. Since male socialization includes an emphasis on female beauty and transient relationships, this finding is not surprising.

Although the possibilities for sustained Eros in a paired relation are rather remote, sometimes the ideal of Eros is fulfilled in real life. Two researchers, Cuber and Harnoff found that such relations occur in perhaps 10 per cent of all marriages.

Ludus (Self Centered) Love

> *Right now I'm involved with two men. They both know about each other. I like having two men around. This way I always have something to do. When one is busy, I see the other one. If I have an argument with one, I still have the other. Some people say this keeps me from working out my problems in relationships and keeps the relationship from getting to a deeper level, but I like it this way. Knowing that someone else is in the picture keeps both of him or her on his or her toes. They never take me for granted. And I don't have to deal with all that love stuff. They know I'm not going to get too serious with either of them. Who needs all that serious stuff anyway? I just want to have a good time.*

In contrast to the erotic lover, the ludic lover views love as a game, refuses to become dependent on any one person, and does not encourage another's intimacy. Like a cat teasing a mouse, the ludic lover keeps the partner at a distance. And while the ludic lover is criticized by the erotic lover because of his/her lack of commitment, moralists condemn the Ludic's implicit promiscuity or hedonism. But the ludic lover explains that to make a game of love does not diminish its value. Skill in playing the game is the issue.

Two skills of every ludic are to juggle several people at the same time and to manage each relationship so that no one is seen too often. These strategies help to ensure that the relationship does not deepen into an all-consuming love. The ludic lover may keep two, three, or even four lovers "on a string" at one time. There are always "backups". Sex is self centered and exploitative rather than symbolic of a relationship.

Don Juan represented the classic ludic lover. To him, the pleasure of the game was in the chase, not in capturing the prize. Once I am sure that a girl has fallen in love with me, I gradually begin to lose interest in her, is a statement that characterizes the ludic lover.

A ludic lover wants sex for fun, not as emotional rapport, and s/he is much more willing to delay sexual satisfaction than is the Eros lover, for whom sex is an integral part of the fascination. Flattery, coyness, coquetry, and gallantry are all part of the ludic strategy and add spice and pleasurable tension to the couple's interaction. Unlike Eros ludic lovers are usually quite content with their detachment from the intense feelings of love and are not jealous or possessive.

The Ludus person does not have a specific vision of ideal beauty, as does the Eros person, but has a wide range of physical tastes, and anyone who falls into this category is considered a desirable partner. As the Ludus man said in Finnian's Rainbow, "when he's not near the girl he loves, he loves the girl he's near." Or, "If You Can't Be With The One You Love, Love The One You're With" (Crosby, Stills, and Nash).

When Ludus people have the misfortune to select an Eros person for a ludic adventure, their attempts to keep the relationship pleasantly casual are usually not successful, and the breakup can be quite painful for the Eros person. However, when the game of Ludus love is played by two people who understand the rules and the expectations, the relation can be ended quite gracefully, especially since each has at least one other backup partner at the same time, and neither expected to obtain a long-lasting satisfactory relationship anyway, but only an interlude of adventure, excitement, and (often) sexual attraction.

Although hopefully changing, in terms of the gender specific stereotypes, as stated, the ludic lover also tends to be a man. It is possible that because women are viewed as objects, men relate to them as to objects and their actions, options, and lives are restricted by rules and limitations applicable to objects. Too many men are preoccupied with the accumulation of many sexual conquests rather than with the development of a warm and deep love relationship with another human being.

Storge (Life Long Friends) Love

Kevin and I have known each other since we were kids. We went through elementary, junior high, and high school together. Our families were very close also. In fact, his sister is like my own sister. As a teenager, if I had an argument with my mother, I would go and complain to Kevin's mother. Kevin and I lost touch during the college years because we both went to different colleges. But then, one night we found ourselves at a mutual friend's party. From that time on, we've been together— first, as boyfriend and girlfriend and then, as husband and wife.

Our relationship has been nice. I wouldn't call it exciting or passionate but we're comfortable together—the kind of comfort that you have when you're with family. Most of the time we know what the other is thinking or feeling without using words—that's how well we know each other. We usually don't argue because we mostly like doing the same things and agree on most important matters. Our sex life—well, that's okay too. Again, not exciting or passionate but comfortable.

Storge (pronounced stor-gay) characterizes the love of friendship, companionship, and affection. Storgic lovers are essentially good friends who have grown in intimacy through close association, with an unquestioned assumption that their relationship will be permanent. Without either partner experiencing feelings of ecstasy, storge lovers have a deep caring for each other. Storge love has a subtle beginning. It is as if the partners remember no specific point when they felt love for each other. Yet there is a deep feeling of intimacy, which binds each to the other.

Storge is an unexciting, uneventful, and impassionate love, quite different from either Ludus or Eros. It is a companionate form of love, a love of quiet affection based on practical considerations with goals of marriage, children, and an established place in the community. The storge lover is practical and predictable. The emotional component of love is low key. Storge lovers plan their relationship- what they will do together every night. Spontaneity is lacking. To the ludic or erotic lover, storge is a bore. But storge love has its advantages.

Whereas erotic lovers study each other's faces and talk endlessly about each other's past lives and current feelings, and are intensely aware of the fact of being in love, storgic lovers treat each other simply as old friends. To Eros or Ludus, Storge is not really love at all. On the other hand, to the Storge person, the playfulness of Ludus is a mockery of serious love and the ecstasy of Eros is a fantasy, an illusion.

Storgic lovers build up a reservoir of stability that will see them through difficulties that would kill a ludic relationship and greatly strain an erotic one. The physical absence of the beloved, for instance, is much less distressing to them than to erotic lovers; they can survive long separations. Also in the ludic relationship, something is happening all the time (a game is being played) and inactivity leads to boredom. In storge, there are fewer campaigns to fight and fewer wounds to heal. Women are more likely to be storge lovers than men, perhaps because female socialization emphasizes caring, companionship, and affection. Other research has also revealed that women tend to be more rational about love.

Sexual intimacy comes late in the slow development of storgic love, not because the Storge person necessarily takes a puritanical attitude toward sexuality, but because s/he considers a rapid progress toward sexual intimacy to be inappropriate. Sex does not become a factor in Storge until after an intellectual and emotional understanding has been achieved, and even then the Storge person does not anticipate emotional intensity. The concept of ecstasy is, of course, completely beyond his/her range of expectations. It is therefore not surprising that sexual disappointment is far less likely to break up the storgic pair than it is an erotic or ludic couple.

Although Storge is rarely hectic or urgent, it is not without its disagreements and conflicts, and storgic partnerships do not always survive. If a breakup does occur, however, the storgic lovers are very likely to remain good friends. It would be inconceivable to a Storge person that two people who had truly loved one another at one time could hate each other simply because they had ceased to be lovers.

By mixing varying degrees of these three styles, Lee derived three secondary styles of loving:

Agape (Thou Centered) Love

Jimmy and I knew each other a year before we were married. He came from a poor family and had worked his way through college. Ever since he was a young boy, he wanted to go to medical school. When I met him, he had just finished sending out his applications to all the top schools. He was accepted by one of his top choices. He was so excited. He didn't have the money for tuition so we had to figure out how he could go. I knew how much he wanted to go to medical school, so I suggested that I would work and pay for his tuition and books. He was so happy. Finally his dream was coming true. It gave me such pleasure to be able to do this for him.

We got married and moved to the university town. It was rough at first. I had to work long hours in order to pay the high tuition rates. In the beginning, we didn't have much time together, with his studying all the time and my working all the time. In fact, for the first two years, it felt like we were two ships passing in the night. We didn't argue because we didn't see each other enough to argue. And our sex life was virtually nil. But it didn't matter because he was finally realizing his dream and I was helping him.

The agapic lover has only the best interests of his/her partner at heart. Such a lover would be more likely to help his/her love object to get medical attention for a venereal disease contracted from someone else than to be angry or punitive toward the love object for having the sexual relationship in the first place. "Whatever I can do to make your life happy" is the motif for the agapic lover, even if this means giving up the beloved to someone else. Neither men nor women are more likely to have an agapic style of love than the other sex.

Mania is the most common combination of Eros and Ludus. The manic lover is racked by yearning and moodiness, alternating between momentary highs of irrational joy and lows of anxiety and depression. The slightest lack of response from the other causes pain and resentment, while any sign of warmth brings enormous relief. The manic lover's pleasure is always short lived, however, since his/her needs for attention and affection are virtually insatiable. S/he seems almost possessed by some strange demon, gripped by a sort of madness, which seizes him/her and produces a torment of unsatisfied desire and humiliation. The manic lover has difficulty functioning without his/her partner. S/he is obsessed with the beloved. Jealousy and inability to sleep eat, or think logically characterize the manic lover. And while the manic lover has peaks of excitement, s/he also experiences the depths of depression.

Mania is the theme of innumerable romantic novels, with their familiar characteristics of extreme jealousy, helpless obsession, and tragic ending. The literature of love portrays the manic lover as a person whose feelings are beyond rational control, and who is swept about by winds of fortune and his/her own self-doubt. Women are more likely to be manic lovers than men. Again, hopefully these stereotypes are changing. Traditionally, women were socialized to be dependent. Even in this country women in the very recent past needed a husband's signature and consent to travel abroad, to own property, to borrow money, or even to work.

Sexual intimacy only brings new problems to the manic lover. Uncertain of his attractiveness and lacking a genuine rapport with the other, the manic lover is unable to participate in a mutually compatible sexual relationship.

Mania (Intense Dependency) Love

Sally was in love with Richie. She said she fell in love with him the first moment she saw him. She was determined to have him as her own. The problem was that Richie was married to someone else. Richie's marriage wasn't too stable; they had grown apart over the years, and Richie had been unhappy for a long time. He was reluctant to get a divorce because he thought it would negatively affect his young daughter.

Sally was divorced for about two years when she first met Richie and she was determined to seduce him. Since they worked together, they had many opportunities to be alone. One night, when they were working late, she virtually attacked him, without too much resistance on his part. They started having an affair. As time went on, Sally became more and more preoccupied with Richie. She would have her friends on the phone for hours discussing the details of their love life, their sex life, and analyzing their relationship. Her friends were sick and tired of the whole thing. They tried to talk sense to Sally but she wouldn't listen to anyone.

If Richie was the least bit distant to Sally, it called for a three-hour conversation about what was going on with him. If he went out on a consultation job, she would question him until he was so frustrated he would want to end the relationship. This would then provoke another conversation that would last until the wee hours of the morning— not to mention the barrage of phone calls he would receive the next day. One night, when he went out on a consultation, she was sure he was seeing another woman. She followed him and confronted him in the parking lot. At this point, he had had about as much as he could take and ended the relationship. Sally sat on the hood of the car and refused to get off until Richie changed his mind. Finally he did and they ended their fight in a motel. Richie then had to explain to his wife why he got home so late from his meeting.

After about three years of the affair, Sally called Richie's wife and told her of their long-standing affair. Richie and his wife got a divorce. Interestingly enough, Richie and Sally married and have been happily together for almost ten years.

It is theoretically possible for a manic attachment to develop into a lasting love, but there are only rare instances of this happening. In order for this relationship to endure, the other person must have the patience and ego strength to ride out the possessiveness, the recriminations, and the storms of emotions. Only an Eros person is likely to do this. A Ludus person would never tolerate the manic lover's extremes and, while a Storge person may try to be kind, s/he would never be able to reciprocate the manic lover's intensity.

Mania rarely ends happily, and most manic lovers remain troubled by the experience for months and even years. A period of hatred of the former partner is almost essential if the lover is finally to achieve an attitude of indifference. During the recovery period, the manic lover is often in a condition popularly known as "the rebound." This period can be very dangerous for any new partner, since the unrequited manic lover is likely to take on a ludic role. Once a successful relationship has been achieved, s/he will very probably drop the new partner, thus evening out the score for his/her prior disappointment. In other words, s/he loved and was not requited and now s/he has been loved and refused to requite. If the new partner is ludic there is no problem of course, but if s/he is manic, the cycle of broken-heart and heart breaker will begin another round.

Most of the manic lovers believe that the experience of falling in love had been profitable despite the pain, since the extremes of manic emotion had enabled them to realize how much they could care for another person.

Pragma (Logical-Sensible) Love

> *Stan and Marie met each other at school. They had both bought new computers and decided to take a computer course to expand their expertise. Although Stan wasn't good looking in the typical sense, he was very practical, hardworking, and frugal. Marie also approached life in a very pragmatic way. She was immediately attracted to Stan when he suggested that instead of dinner out, he would cook for her. It was so expensive these days to eat out. For Christmas, he bought her new tires for her car, which she needed desperately. She bought him a new air conditioner because his had broken.*
>
> *Now, three years later, Marie was still comfortable in her decision to marry Stan. So, he wasn't someone she was physically attracted to, sex with him was tolerable. And, on occasion, she almost enjoyed it. While their relationship was not passionate, they enjoyed doing many things together like planting a vegetable garden. Last summer, they planted, jarred, and froze enough vegetables to last through the winter. Think about how much money they saved. Some of Marie's friends felt sad every time they saw her. They thought she had missed out. Marie only felt that way sometimes because Stan was a good provider and was very responsible and dependable.*

Women are more likely to be pragmatic than men in their love relationships. Pragmatic lovers are more likely to look realistically at their own assets, decide on their "market value" and set off to get the best possible "deal" in their partners. The pragmatic lover remains loyal and faithful and defines his/her status as "in love" as long as the loved one is perceived as a "good bargain" (Hatkoff and Lasswell). Such rationality is similar to that of the storgic lover who also tends to be a woman. Women traditionally have been taught to seek husbands who are "good providers" since women themselves have not been reared to become economically self-sufficient.

Lovers who represent the pure forms of Eros, lupus, storge, agape, mania, and pragma are difficult to find. Most people have some elements of each. In fact, it is probably true that although there are many types of love between a couple in a paired relation, they are all blends of three major categories: Eros, Ludus, and Storge. This formulation helps explain the difficulty of understanding the love of another couple (What does she see in him?) as well as the pain and puzzlement that occurs when a person characterized by one type of love attempts to relate to a person characterized by another type. For one of the most important contributions of this research is that, although each person defines true love in terms of his/her own experience; this experience can be completely different for each person.

There are endless possible combinations of the major types of love, so that the experience of love may be infinitely varied. Moreover the person's typology of love is not necessarily fixed for the whole of his/her life or even for the duration of the specific paired relation. In addition, s/he may experience love in one relation quite differently from the way s/he does in another. However, s/he will usually be characterized within a rather narrow range in terms of his/her concept, experience, and ideal of love.

To complicate the matter even further, the type of love relationship that one chooses may differ across the life cycle. Early on, in late adolescence or young adulthood, a person may opt for romantic love and sexual chemistry. At a somewhat older age, during the childrearing years, this very same person may want a stable, responsible person, someone who could be a good provider and good mother/father to the children. Someone who has finished childrearing may choose a companion, a friend, with whom to share experiences.

Given the bewildering varieties of love that may occur with a blend of the three major categories of Eros, Ludus, and Storge, it is not surprising that disappointments in love frequently occur. A person who regards his/her own definition of love as the only "true" or valid one will be puzzled or impatient when s/he encounters examples that do not fit his/her preconceptions. Further, s/he may be devastated by his/her failure to relate to someone whose expectations for love are completely different from his/her own. On the other hand, a person who is aware of the many forms that "true love" may take is likely to be much more flexible and thus have an enormous advantage in wending his/her way successfully through the maze of an intimate relationship.

4   HOW DO YOU LEARN TO LOVE?

"You learn to love your Mom and Dad because your Mom and Dad take care of each other— take care of you. You learn that they're your Mom and Dad and you learn to love them because they take care of you." Brian.

The ability to give and receive love depends on a number of factors. Probably the most important factor is the amount of love the person received as a child and his/her level of personal maturity and adjustment as an adult. Researcher Horn found that adults who grew up in "love poor" families typically placed less value on love and more on material goods than those who had received a lot of love during childhood. This finding held whether the children's families were poor or well off. Furthermore, individuals who are immature and maladjusted have difficulty in love relationships because they bring their problems with them and inevitably complicate if not destroy such relationships. Finally, persons who are low in self-esteem often consider themselves unworthy of love and find it hard to believe that someone else can accept them or love them. They may even try to prove they are unlovable by sabotaging any burgeoning relationships.

However, even long-held patterns of insulation and low self-esteem can sometimes be dissipated by the experience of being genuinely loved by another human being and by learning to love in return. Curiously enough, it is often when a person seems least worthy of love and acceptance that s/he needs it the most. It usually takes a rewarding person—a person who communicates an attitude of love, attraction, acceptance, appreciation, encouragement, and commitment—to break through the defenses of an "unlovable" person and bring out the best in him/her.

The emotion of love is first experienced in infancy as a result of receiving nurture, usually from the mother (or caretaking person). As infants passively receive food and are held and fondled, they come to identify the resultant satisfaction with themselves and to perceive themselves as an object of worth- an object that is associated with the experience of deep and positive need satisfaction. It may be said that they come to love themselves —in the sense that we have defined the term love (a positive emotion that occurs when an important need is gratified). Apparently infants must have this first experience of themselves as a love object before they can experience love in relation to other.

Persons who lack this initial experience of love will, as they mature, try to compensate for this lack of self-love by demonstrating a greedy self-interest, by perceiving others chiefly in terms of their usefulness, and by manipulating them for their own gain. This is termed selfishness, which is the antithesis of self-love.

Most people think that selfish persons are self-satisfied and do exactly as they please. Closer observation, however, shows that "selfish" persons are generally anxiously concerned with themselves, they tend to be never satisfied, are usually restless, always driven by a fear of not getting enough, of missing something, of being deprived of something. They are filled with burning envy of anyone who might have more, If we observe them still closer, we find that these persons are basically not fond of themselves but deeply dislike themselves (Eric Fromm). In contrast, persons operating from a firm base of self-love will extend their sense of self-acceptance and self -regard to the acceptance and regard of significant others.

The infant's first significant other, or love object (other than himself) is usually the mother, or caretaker, who is of course the figure s/he most closely and most often experiences in receiving nurture. Other members of the immediate family and other persons who actively provide nurture will also become love objects as the experience of the child broadens. In addition, inanimate objects (stuffed animals, dolls) and pets may receive the Child's early feelings of loyalty, devotion, and concern and may provide him/her with intense satisfaction.

Infants are completely dependent on their love relation, supplying nothing and taking everything. But as they perceive others as loving, they begin to perceive others as lovable and to provide these others with the nurture and regard that they themselves first received. Extending their sense of self-acceptance or self-love to include a wider social environment than their family, the children begin to demonstrate an independence in relations that becomes increasingly evident from ages 3 to 5. Dependency needs will remain, but they decrease in relative importance. They come to accept age-mates and to form bonds of affection and regard with them. At first sexually neutral, their love for age mates soon focuses especially on same-sexed companions, because in our society, boys are encouraged to play with boys, and girls with girls. Usually, with the advent of puberty (or in some cases, even earlier), this pattern is expected to change; and the adolescent usually begins to form other-sexed primary relations whose intensity of emotional involvement will gradually increase, becoming, through dating, deeply significant paired relations. These relations often are marked by an upsurge of dependency needs that occur simultaneously with adolescents' strong need for independence from the family environment.

With adulthood, the focus of relationship shifts to the need for interdependency. The young adult is then expected to fall in love exclusively with one other-sexed person, abandoning, for the most part, his like-sexed paired relations of childhood and early adolescence, and beginning the cycle again by marrying and providing his/her offspring with the love that s/he received as a child. Thus all three needs—dependency, independence, and interdependency—are present in a person from early childhood, but the emphasis in these needs shifts from dependency to independency to interdependency as the person proceeds through the developmental stages from infancy to adolescence to maturity. Infantile love follows the principle: I love you because I need you. Mature love says: I need you because I love you.

In Freud's psychosexual theory of development, the earliest stage of development, which chiefly entails self-love is known as the narcissistic period, after the Greek myth about Narcissus who fell in love with his reflection in the still waters of a pool. In the second stage, which Freud termed the Oedipal stage, after the Greek myth of Oedipus, love is focused chiefly on the mother, and the father is seen as a rival.

The time period when love is experienced chiefly with members of the same sex is known as the latency period and extends from about the ages of eight to twelve years. This period is followed by the heterosexual or genital period, characterized by mature adolescence through maturity. The adult period characterized by mature love, with the emphasis on giving, or providing rather than receiving, completes the circle, with the adult now providing nurture and affection for his/her mate and his children.

Persons may be fixated or stuck at any of the psychosexual stages and remain oriented chiefly to the characteristics of that stage. This is termed fixation. For example, the adult, though fully developed physically, socially and economically, may still be narcissistic, or incapable of any but self-love (while the severely disturbed adult may not be capable even of that). Or, a person fixated at the latency stage may never proceed to the heterosexual stage. Similarly, a fixation at the heterosexual stage may limit the capacity of a person for mature love. (This is not to imply that mature love is the exclusive province of the heterosexual. Both the homosexual and the heterosexual are capable of proceeding to mature love, if mature love is defined as an emphasis on giving rather than receiving.)

It must not be assumed of course that a person proceeds from stage to stage in discrete jumps. Each stage blends into the other. Moreover, as the person proceeds through the psychosexual developmental stages, it is the emphasis on experience that changes; elements of all preceding stages remain. Thus an adult characterized by mature love still retains the elements of narcissistic love for example as a base on which other elements are established—such as love of mother, father, family, friends, mate, and children.

EXERCISE: The Genogram

On sheets of paper, draw out your family tree, going back three generations. This would include you, your parents, and your grandparents. Try to include as many family members as possible, i.e. your brothers, sisters and their children. If you are married and have children, you might want to include your children, your generation, your parents, and your grandparents. Use squares to indicate the males and circles to indicate the females. Keep all the generations on the same line.

Next. Include any significant personality traits, relationships etc. For example, obesity, divorce, alcoholism, mental illness. Indicate strong relationships and conflicted ones.

See if you can find any patterns. For example, first-born males in your father's family were all alcoholics or drug users. Or, first born females in your mother's family all had non-traditional careers. Write down the patters you find below. Compare your notes with your partner.

EXERCISE: Important Caretakers

Once you have finished the genogram, you might want to explore the
following questions in your journal:

1. What did your mother teach you about women?

_____

_____

_____

2. What did your mother teach you about men?

_____

_____

_____

3. What did your father teach you about women?

_____

_____

_____

4. What did your father teach you about men?

_____

_____

_____

5. What did your mother teach you about relationships?

_____

_____

_____

6. What did your father teach you about relationships?

_____

_____

_____

7. What did your mother teach you about sex?

_____

_____

_____

8. What did your father teach you about sex?

_____

_____

_____

9. What are the best and worst qualities of your mother?

_____

_____

_____

10. What are best and worst qualities of your father?

_____

_____

_____

11. What best qualities of both your parents are in you?

_____

_____

12. What worst qualities of both your parents are in you?

_____

_____

_____

13. What best qualities of both your parents are in your partner?

_____

_____

_____

14. What worst qualities of both your parents are in your partner?

_____

_____

_____

5

WHAT ARE THE PSYCHOLOGICAL CONDITIONS NECESSARY FOR LOVE?

"Well, this might be wrong but it might be feelings, friendship, sticking up for each other, liking loving each other. Uhm, I think that's it. Like really knowing that you love each other." Brian.

Positive Self-Concept:

The way we feel about ourselves is our self-concept. A positive self-concept is one in which we like ourselves and enjoy being who we are. A person who has achieved a genuine self-acceptance can say:

> *This is what I am. I am no more, no less. I am sometimes wise and sometimes foolish. I am sometimes brave and sometimes cowardly. I am caring and uncaring. I am moral and immoral. I am sometimes the best and sometimes the worst. I am all these things. I do not approve of everything I am, but that doesn't prevent me from recognizing and accepting myself for what I am.*

A positive self-concept is important since once we accept ourselves, we can believe that others are capable of doing so too. In contrast, a negative self-concept has devastating consequences for the individual and those persons with whom s/he becomes involved. Individuals who cannot accept themselves tend to reject others. They make the assumption, if s/he wants me, there must be something wrong with him/her. Or as Groucho Marx said, "I wouldn't want to belong to a country club who would have me as a member."

The way we feel about ourselves and our ability to relate intimately are both learned. Our first potential love relationships were with our parents or the person(s) who cared about us in infancy. As babies, we were literally helpless. When we were hungry, cold or wet, we cried until someone came to take care of us. Our parents became associated with reducing our discomfort. When we saw them, we knew that everything would be okay.

Being well cared for as infants helps establish a good self-concept by teaching us that we are somebody that someone else cares about, and that other people are good because they do things (feed, get blanket, change diaper) which make us feel good. Once we learn as young children to love and to trust the people we live with, then we can generalize this lesson to others and eventually establish adult relationships.

Self-Disclosure:

Self-Disclosure is essential in building romantic relationships. And couples in love do tend to reveal a great deal about themselves to one another. Such disclosures greatly increase vulnerability to hurt, although they help couples to become closer and to understand each other better. People must be willing to disclose their feelings to others if they want to love and be loved. One who does not disclose himself/herself truthfully and fully can never love another person nor can s/he be loved by the other person. Effective loving calls for knowledge of the loved object. "How can I love a person whom I do not know? How can the person love me if s/he does not know me?"

It is not easy for us to let others know who we are, what we feel, or what goes on inside our heads. We often fear that, if others really knew what we were thinking, they might be less admiring or less respectful or they might think we were crazy. "I might be rejected as a friend or lover." Or, "If they really knew me, the wouldn't like me." Since such withdrawals would be painful, we protect our relationships and ourselves by allowing others to know only certain facets of who we are.

Trust is the condition under which people are willing to disclose themselves. In order to feel comfortable about letting someone else inside your heads, you must feel whatever feelings or information we share will not be judged and will be safe with that person. This implies that self-disclosure occurs in relationships with people who are protective of us (not destructive), and with people who are deeply concerned (not resentful or rejecting) about us. If a trust is betrayed, a person may become bitterly resentful and vow never to disclose him or herself again.

Social Skills:

In addition to a positive self-concept and the ability to self-disclose, those who develop love relationships with ease often have an array of social skills. They have good eye contact, they smile, and they initiate conversations and express an interest in the other person.

6

IS THERE SUCH A THING AS LOVE AT FIRST SIGHT?

> *Love walked right in and drowned the shadows away*
> *Love walked right in and brought my sunniest day*
> *One magic moment and my heart seemed to know*
> *That love said hello ...*
> *(Harry and Sally)*

"DEFINITELY NOT! DEFINITELY NOT! No, you don't know what they're like. Maybe you see this hot, really nice girl that's real pretty and she's on drugs, or she has AIDS, or she has cancer. Or maybe she's on patrol— the thing that when you're arrested you can't violate ..." Brian.

> *I fell in love with a man I met last month at a weeklong conference. When I first saw him, it was like no one else was in the room. We were drawn to each other like magnets. He sat down next to me and we started talking. I could hardly speak because my heart was pounding so. We had to keep reminding ourselves to be quiet and to listen to the speaker. We were so comfortable with each other; it felt like we had known each other forever. That night we made passionate, wonderful love— all night. For the remainder of the week, we couldn't bear to be apart. Every time we were near each other, we wanted to touch each other, kiss each other, and make love with each other.*
>
> *Since that week, our phone bills have become astronomical. We spend hours on the phone reminiscing about our times together, how it felt to be with each other, how it will be again, etc. Since we live in different parts of the country, we take turns flying to each other's homes.*

One element that characterizes love at first sight is an immediate, strong attraction to another person. In some cases, this attraction may be almost entirely physical. In the above example, the tone of the person's voice, the look in his eyes when he spoke to her evoked a response that was more intense than she had remembered experiencing before. In some such affairs, the attraction is mutual; both are aware almost from the moment of their meeting of a response to each other that exerts a compulsive pull toward physical intimacy.

In other cases, the immediate attraction may arise more predominantly from the fact that the two see in each other's appearance or manner, or in the circumstances under which they meet, the "ideal" they have been looking for in a mate. Chance may bring about their meeting at a moment in their lives when both are in an attitude of openness and readiness to embrace the embodied "ideal." This second factor, perhaps, operates in love at-first-sight affairs more often than specific sexual attraction does.

What brings people to the point of emotional readiness to fall in love at first sight is an interesting question. Sometimes there is a particular need at the moment to escape from certain problems in the circumstances of life or in one's own emotional life. Emotional or material complications may exert a strong pressure toward sudden falling in love. It is possible that there have been a number of people who fall suddenly in love when confronted with a crisis in life or with the necessity for making a major choice or decision. When the time comes that one must go on to the next thing such as at the end of the college years or after the death of a parent or loved one, love offers an out that is not publicly disapproved; rather it is an out that society even approves and looks upon with sentimental fondness.

At such a time two people meet and it makes little difference whether the immediate mutual attraction is chiefly physical or whether it is a response to a conception of an ideal. In either event, the resulting flare up is what is known as love at first sight. The urge is to make strong bonds without delay. If such a couple marries at once, their marriage might accidentally be a compatible union. It has about the same chance for success as any other unpremeditated, wild plunge has for producing a happy outcome. But some couples so attracted to each other proceed cautiously and become well acquainted. They take time to discover each other's attitudes, beliefs, habits and tastes. Some such couples scarcely know at what point in their association they pass the phase of rather superficial attraction and progress into a relationship enriched by other elements necessary to lasting love. If, on becoming better acquainted with each other, they had discovered no sound basis of congeniality, the early attraction would have had little chance to survive.

7 WHAT'S THE DIFFERENCE BETWEEN LOVE AND INFATUATION?

Couple 1.

Amy looked at John as he walked up from the lake. They were dating about two years now. She remembered when she first met him. It was at a friend's house. He was her friend's brother's college roommate who was visiting for the weekend. She liked the way he looked from the beginning— medium height, brownish hair and big gray-brown sparkly eyes. He had an easy way about him, comfortable and calm. Sometimes he would toss his head to the side to get the hair out of his eyes. He still tossed his hair out of his eyes and she still liked the way he looked.

While she was waiting for her friend to get ready, they started talking about different courses they were taking at college. She was impressed by his intelligence and boyish ways. He seemed able to speak intelligently about various topics and then in the next breath show her his clever sense of humor. As the years passed, it was his sense of humor that got them past the few arguments they did have. She would be fuming mad about something and he would say, "C'mon Amy, we both love each other. Then he would do something funny and make her laugh. She could never stay angry with him for long.

She seemed to feel a sense of calm when he was around. Sometimes she just liked to watch him when he didn't know she was watching. She liked to watch him concentrating on a math problem or when he was deep in thought. Then, sensing that she was watching him, he would turn around quickly and break out in a big smile. At those times, she would go over and give him a hug and every thing felt simply okay. They liked doing little things for each other—making each other laugh or smile, making little funny pictures on their notes to each other. They cared about each other. She worried about him when he had the flu last year and had a high fever. She just wanted him to get better. At one point, right before exams, she worried because she thought he wasn't getting enough sleep. Another time, he worried about her because he felt she was worrying too much about him. Their sex life was good. Her heart still skipped a beat when they kissed. She liked the way his skin felt, the way he tasted, the way he felt, the way he touched her. It was mainly that they felt good together. They really liked and cared about each other.

Couple 2.

Christine and Jack have been seeing each other for about two years. They met in a doctor's office. Waiting for their turn, they started talking and hit it off right away. He waited until she finished her appointment and they went out for coffee. That night they went back to her apartment and barely made it through the door before they made love. Since then, they have been seeing each other on a regular basis.

They see each other about two times a week, either going out for a movie or dinner. Most of the times, though, they order Chinese food and eat it in bed before making love. Most of their time together is spent in heavy discussion about feelings and their relationship. Often, Christine will greet him at the door saying, "We have to talk about 'us'." It's getting to the point where he cringes every time she says "us." This usually precipitates a deep exploration into his and her feelings about a particular topic, issue or event. After the discussion, they usually wind up making intense, passionate love. He then leaves early the next morning. If he leaves too early or isn't as attentive as she wants him to be, she gets angry and calls him at work to discuss her feelings.

Christine would like to see Jack more but he's reluctant to do so. He doesn't want to get into a deep, committed relationship. She gets angry with this and often they spend a good deal of time arguing about why he won't spend more time with her. Each time they're together, they are passionately involved with each other—either by screaming and yelling at each other or having sex with each other. They have broken up for short periods of time on several occasions, only to get back together again in an intense way.

Christine feels like she's making progress in the relationship because Jack has consented to stay over for an entire weekend next month. He consented to this after three hours of her asking why he couldn't spend more time with her. She can't understand why, if he has the day off, he can't spend it with her. Or, why, if he has an extra hour at work, why he can't call her. Also, even though she had to remind him three times, he bought her two presents for her birthday. Now she is convinced that he's caring more about her.

Sometimes, when he doesn't call for a few days, Christine thinks he might have another girlfriend.

Looking at the above two couples, it seems obvious to us which couple is in love and which couple is in infatuation. But if we asked all four individuals, they might all tell us that they were in love. Many writers like to distinguish between love and infatuation. Most believe the two emotions are different, but no one is quite sure in what way. Infatuation is generally viewed with suspicion as being a kind of love that will lead the follower down the path of disillusionment. Infatuation is often described as being on a lower level than love and unworthy of marriage. Rarely, however, does the individual involved define a current emotional experience as infatuation. Whenever individuals speak of their infatuation, it is nearly always in the past tense. Very few individuals report themselves as being currently infatuated, yet at a given time a fair number will consider themselves to be in love.

Apparently when individuals are going through the emotional relationship, they call it love; when it's over, they often call it infatuation. By calling past love affairs infatuations, the individual maintains the uniqueness of love, so that when s/he falls in love at some future time, the term love will refer to the new relationship, not the used one that didn't work. Many individuals however will admit to having been in love on several occasions. The concept of infatuation seems to be of little analytical value for anyone trying to understand love. Because of its ex post facto nature, it is useful only for categorizing past love relationships, not for understanding present or future ones. It is useful to employ the term infatuation to distinguish an emotion which in many respects is similar to love (especially romantic love), but which should be differentiated from love. Both infatuation and love are based on a need to experience an intimate emotional and tactile relation with a love object. But infatuation has little to do with the reality of the personality of the highly idealized love object, since the idealization is based chiefly on fantasy.

There are two types of infatuation objects:

- The distant infatuation object, whom the person knows not at all, or knows slightly (for example, political or entertainment figures, or athletic heroes), and
- the associative infatuation object, whom the person knows and dates. An associative infatuation can involve a very deep intimate relationship, which nonetheless is not love.

Infatuation tends to focus on a single perceived characteristic of the infatuation object, such as voice or appearance, which in some cases may even acquire the force of a fetish. Love however focuses on the whole person as a love object. Whereas an infatuated person tends to relate to the object of his/her infatuation as an object to be manipulated, controlled, or used, a person in love relates to his/her love object by identifying him/herself with it. Further, this identification with the love object tends to be persistent and enduring, while the relation to an infatuation object tends to be fickle and rather short-lived.

Infatuation is self-centered; love is other-centered. An infatuated person tends to be preoccupied with him/herself and his/her own feelings; s/he often feels awkward, constrained, self-conscious, unfulfilled, fragmented, and insecure. S/he may withdraw from sensory experience and contact with others, becoming less and less aware of incoming stimuli (s/he may daydream, stay away from friends, be unable to eat). On the other hand, a person in love is oriented toward the well being of the love object and tends to be less self-conscious or concerned with him/her self and with feelings of difficulty and inadequacy. S/he feels relatively more self-assured, secure, and personally adequate. S/he is active and open to sensory experience. S/he feels healthy and alive. S/he delights in all aspects of his/her environment— food, friends, sights, and sounds. S/he is moved to put his/her dreams into action. In other words, infatuation binds energy, love releases energy. The person in love functions more efficiently, with greater drive, increased awareness, and an eagerness for achievement.

Because of our society's emphasis on the importance of romantic love, the young person in our society dreams of the fulfillment of love s/he is ready for or even encounters an appropriate object of romantic love. The person will often experience infatuation as a temporary fulfillment of his/her culturally conditioned need for a romantic love experience. And since the emotional and physical manifestations of love and infatuation are, on the surface, comparable, s/he is able to define his/her experience as love.

These initial infatuation experiences also provide a kind of training ground for love. The young person is able to experience and assess the vicarious fulfillments of a distant infatuation object, who is safely remote, anonymous, and undemanding, and second, the problems, disappointments, and fulfillments of an associative infatuation object, who is available and who makes demands. In the second real experience, s/he usually discovers eventually (and to his/her disappointment) that the infatuation object is not a love object; that s/he has created this object out of his/her own self centered fantasies, that s/he is unwilling and indeed unable to fulfill the demands and needs of the object, and that s/he is merely exploiting this object for the fulfillment of emotions that are immature. S/he discovers that romantic love, unlike infatuation, involves a paired relation, which is intimate, personal, giving, as well as receiving, and real. The other in a love relation is an individual rather than the personification of a fantasy ideal.

Thus, infatuation will often precede love. With increasing maturity, a person may shift from the energy binding, self-centered, withdrawn, unrealistic, and manipulative characteristics of infatuation to the energy releasing, other centered, outgoing, unselfconscious, and altruistic characteristics of love.

Gary and Sheila both divorced and in their forties, dated seriously for four years. Both were professionals and had joint custody of their children. They believed they were in love. They shared many activities, both leisure and professional, and hoped that eventually they would marry. At least this was their initial feeling about their relationship. As time passed, Gary relaxed around being attentive to Sheila and Sheila began to verbally criticize Gary. In spite of this, they had an intense, good sex life. Sheila felt that Gary would ultimately abandon her as did her father so she had unconsciously rejected him (through her criticisms) before this could occur. Her criticisms activated Gary's feelings of not being good enough. As a result, he would then often withdraw, triggering Sheila's fears of abandonment. And so the cycle went on.

Eventually Gary was attracted to Susan, a young woman who idolized and adored him. They began an affair. Feeling very guilty, Gary told Sheila and now Sheila's worst fears were realized. She was abandoned. But, in so doing, Gary had provided her with material (the affair), for which she could criticize him forever— for now as far as Sheila was concerned, Gary could never be good enough. And in so doing, they both reenacted their childhood scripts.

8 WHAT'S THE DIFFERENCE BETWEEN LIKING AND LOVING?

"Well, love is, uhm, love is when you really like someone. You <u>really</u> have a crush on them. It's when you <u>really</u> like each other. Like you <u>REALLY</u> like each other. A LOT! I mean ALOT! And that's love. When it's extremely, you love a person. And like is when you like them like a friend, Like, I like you. Well, actually, I love you. Like my friend Scott. Well, I like him. I don't love him. I like him as a friend." Brian.

What is the difference between liking someone and loving someone? Sociologist Rubin developed two scales: one to measure loving and one to measure liking. While he found the basic components of romantic love to be attachment, caring, and intimacy, he found the basic components of liking to be affection and respect. Liking based on affection is experienced as emotional warmth and closeness; liking based on respect is experienced as admiration. Both components are usually found in friendship.

He concluded that a moderate amount of liking is probably a prerequisite for establishing a love relationship. He noted however that although liking and loving have much in common, he would hesitate to equate the two. People often express liking for a person whom they would not claim to love in the least. In other instances, they may declare their love for someone whom they cannot reasonably be said to like very well. Thus, while Rubin considers liking and loving to be related, he nevertheless sees them as distinctly different emotions.

This distinction between liking and loving becomes important when we try to figure out how we really feel about another person—whether we are dealing with liking, with companionate love, with romantic love, or with some combination.

The development of love often involves a range of different types of love feelings. These include liking, loving, and what is referred to as romantic love.

Liking:

"I never met a man I didn't like," humorist Will Rogers once said. We understand and use the word like as he did to imply affection and respect. We have feelings of affection toward those who relate to us in a friendly way. "From the day my roommate asked me if I wanted to go shopping with her, we hit it off." Her feelings emphasize the affectionate element of liking. In addition to affection, liking implies respect that is based on a person's admirable characteristics or actions in spheres other than personal relations. Our respect for another person's courage, integrity, or skill may predispose us to like them.

Loving:

While affection and respect comprise the basic elements of liking, attachment, caring, and intimacy help to describe the phenomenon of loving. Attachment refers to a compelling desire to be with another, to make physical contact with them and in general to experience the feeling of being emotionally involved with the other person.

In addition to attachment, loving includes caring. An infant may be attached to its mother, but it is incapable of caring, which implies a more mature form of love. Caring means being concerned about what happens to another. When Rhett Butler said to Scarlet O'Hara in Gone With the Wind, Frankly my dear, I don't give a damn; he was not expressing a key element of his love, his caring.

Beyond attachment and caring, loving implies intimacy. As has already been suggested, intimacy is both a basic reason for our seeking the love experience and a condition for it. As an element of love, intimacy involves the feeling of relating to another, soul to soul. "My partner is the only one who really knows who I am and what I think. The feelings of closeness, of belonging, of sharing make me feel euphoric," said one person.

Romantic and Realistic Love:

As stated earlier, romantic love is different from both liking and loving. It is characterized by such beliefs as love at first sight, there is only one true love, and love is the most important criteria for getting married.

Romantic love is usually described in contrast to realistic love or conjugal love— the love between settled, domestic people. Partners who know all about each other, yet still love each other, are said to have a realistic type of love.

"Well you go out on a few dates and you just learn. You just know each other better. Let's just say I had a girlfriend. I DON'T! But say, I have a girl and she's my friend. She's not my girlfriend. And then I just ask her out on a date, okay? And then we go out on five dates, and we really like each other. Well, that's like being a girlfriend. Then you have to really like or love each other." Brian.

"I think the first thing is that you start out having a crush on somebody. Then you get your friend to find out if she likes you. Maybe your friend does that. Cause my friend does that. He has a crush on her and I'm like his messenger. He sends me to listen to her. I'm like the only one who knows and I'm not telling. I'm the only person who knows who he has a crush on." Brian.

The Love Attitude Inventory (LAI) is a scale that measures your tendency exhibit certain types of behavior in your love relationship. It will give you a score indicating your strongest tendency in your love relationships. Circle the strength of agreement on each sentence.

This is an 18-item measure of love attitudes. Respondents answer each item using a 5-point scale, ranging from 1 (strongly agree), 2 (moderately agree), 3 (neutral), 4 (moderately disagree), 5 (strongly disagree).

The subscales represent 6 different love styles:

EROS (passionate love)

LUDUS (game-playing love)

STORGE (friendship love)

PRAGMA (practical love)

MANIA (possessive, dependent love)

AGAPE (altruistic love)

Scale:

1. My partner and I have the right physical "chemistry" between us.

         1   2   3   4   5

2. I feel that my lover and I were meant for each other.

         1   2   3   4   5

3. My partner fits my ideal standards of physical beauty/handsomness.

         1   2   3   4   5

4. I believe that what my partner doesn't know about me won't hurt him/her.

         1   2   3   4   5

5. I have sometimes had to keep my partner from finding out about other lovers.

         1   2   3   4   5

6. My partner would get upset if he/she knew of some of the things I've done with other people.

    1   2   3   4   5

7. Our love is the best kind because it grew out of a long friendship.

    1   2   3   4   5

8. Our friendship merged gradually into love over time.

    1   2   3   4   5

9. Our love relationship is the most satisfying because it developed from a good friendship.

    1   2   3   4   5

10. A main consideration in choosing my partner was how he/she would reflect on my family.

    1   2   3   4   5

11. An important factor in choosing my partner was whether or not he/she would be a good parent.

    1   2   3   4   5

12. One consideration in choosing my partner was how he/she would reflect on my career.

    1   2   3   4   5

13. When my partner doesn't pay attention to me, I feel sick all over.

    1   2   3   4   5

14. I cannot relax if I suspect that my partner is with someone else.

    1   2   3   4   5

15. If my partner ignores me for a while, I sometimes do stupid things to try to get his/her attention back.

       1   2   3   4   5

16. I would rather suffer myself than let my partner suffer.

       1   2   3   4   5

17. I cannot be happy unless I place my partner's happiness before my own.

       1   2   3   4   5

18. I am usually willing to sacrifice my own wishes to let my partner achieve his/hers.

       1   2   3   4   5

Scoring:

Each subscale is measured separately (each participant gets a different score on each subscale). The items are divided into subscales in the following way:

Eros: 1-3

Ludus: 4-6

Storge: 7-9

Pragma: 10-12

Mania: 13-15

Agape: 16-18

Using the Love Attitude Inventory, several studies have been conducted to find out the degree to which various categories of people are romantic or realistic. When one hundred unmarried men and one hundred unmarried women college students completed the Love Attitude Inventory, the results revealed that men were more romantic than women and that freshmen were more romantic than seniors. Since traditionally, marriage has been more important to women than to men, the women's more realistic attitude toward love was not surprising. The higher realism scores for seniors were expected because they are older and theoretically had been exposed more to the reality of love relationships.

Another study compared the love attitudes of fifty men and fifty women high school seniors with fifty husbands and fifty wives who had been married over twenty years. Both groups revealed a romantic attitude toward love. These findings had been expected for the high school seniors, but not for the older marrieds. One explanation of the findings suggests that those who have been married for twenty years may be expected to adopt attitudes consistent with such a long-term investment of their time and energy. The belief that there is only one person with whom an individual can really fall in love and marry provides cognitive dissonance for those who have done so. When these high school seniors and older marrieds were compared with one hundred young couples (married less than five years), the latter proved very realistic in their attitudes. For them, moonlight and roses had become daylight and dishes. They had been married too long to believe that. As long as you really love a person, you will be able to solve the problems you have with that person, but not long enough to experience the feeling that, "You only really love once."

9

WHAT ARE SOME IMPORTANT COMPONENTS OF LOVE?

The kind of love experience that can be the basis for an enduring lifetime relationship includes some specific components. The thoughtful person looking forward to a permanent commitment to the loved one can consider these factors and assess the potential durability of a relationship. In our culture, one must, in order to assess a love realistically, disregard or deny much of the kind of "love propaganda" to which all young people are exposed in movies, magazines, television, and commercial advertisements of products. All these media present definitions of love that may be distorted and misleading.

Love: Motivation Toward Cooperation

When two people love each other, they have a motivation that enables them to cope with problems and potential frustrations of living in partnership rather than as completely independent individuals. They are motivated to work at the cooperation that is an essential part of love.

The motivation to cooperate is strong in lovers for several reasons. First, the relationship with the loved one is a chosen relationship, chosen because the two find each other attractive and meet at least some of each other's needs. In this way it is different from love relationships with members of one's family, which are thrust upon one without choice. When a person has chosen another and has committed him/herself to loving the chosen one, there is a strong urge to prove the rightness of choice, to "make it work," even if doing so requires adjustment and cooperation that might be withheld or unwillingly given in other relationships. The rightness of one's own perceptions and judgments is at stake.

Perhaps a stronger motivation toward cooperation and adjustability is based on the fact that the love relationship brings security and reassurance to the individual. One feels deeply, whether consciously or not, that the emotional support that comes as a result of loving and being loved is worth working for and, if necessary, sacrificing to maintain. The emotionally healthy person becomes willing to adjust and change when necessary for the sake of such a cooperative relationship.

Cooperative adjustment may be lacking in relationships that are based on the needs of one and that do not have the potential for meeting enough of the needs of both to be permanent. In a problematic relationship, compliance is likely to be required, rather than cooperation offered: "If you love me, you will do what I want," and its counterpart, "If you loved me, you wouldn't ask anything of me." These attitudes mean in reality, "I can think only of my own wants and needs, and I'll use love as a means of coercion."

Companionship: As a Part of Love:

In a love that is adequate for a lifetime of marriage, it is more important that the two be congenial friends. This does not mean that both have to like to fish or go camping, although if they like doing the same things, their friendship-love will be more rewarding. But it is essential that they share feelings about some values that matter most to them both.

Burgess and Locke, two social scientists, made the point that sharing in intellectual, religious, artistic, or altruistic interests means more to a relationship than a sharing in matters such as athletic interests or other general activities that might involve a smaller part of the whole personality.

A man and a woman who love each other should be friends in the same sense that any two people of the same sex are friends. This means they enjoy each other's company because of genuine congeniality, aside from sexual interest; they want to confide in each other, to talk things over, and to share amusement, ideas, disappointment, or grief. They tend to see life through each other's eyes. They are at ease with each other comfortable like two good friends.

Two people who are not at ease and comfortable with each other do not remain close friends. They seek other, more congenial company.

10

WHY IS LOVE SOMETIMES CALLED PARADOXICAL?

Love relationships bring many seeming paradoxes - problems that convey a sense of both conflict and irony, such as the high vulnerability to emotional hurt that accompanies the ecstasy and joy of romantic love.

Separateness and Togetherness:

One of the basic paradoxes of romantic love is that of being a part of a romantic union and simultaneously retaining one's own separate identity and freedom to grow as a person. Researcher Solomon believes that love is ... the taut line of opposed desires between the ideal of an eternal merger of souls and our cultivated urge to prove ourselves as free and autonomous individuals. No matter how much we are in love, there is always a large and nonnegotiable part of ourselves which is not defined by our love world, nor do we want it to be.

Romantic love does not and should not give one person ownership of another. Yet, some lovers make exorbitant demands on their partners' time, attention and effort. They want their partners to drop all outside interests and focus their lives on them. In essence, they want to possess their partners. Often, of course, lovers feel that their great love for their partners justifies such demands. Unfortunately, however, such engulfing love is not great but little. The demanding partner does not really care that much about the well being of the other; rather, s/he is concerned primarily with meeting his/her own dependency or other needs. This is the type of love described earlier by Lee called obsessive or manic loving. The target of this great love is likely to feel a sense of suffocation at being so "lovingly" possessed.

Writer Branden suggests that people in clinging, dependent relationships will see their love die, whereas those in relationships in which both partners are autonomous are better able to keep their love alive. Autonomy indicates a secure sense of self-esteem, so that the person's feelings are not easily hurt over minor conflicts. Immature, dependent individuals tend to translate such minor incidents into evidence of rejection. Between autonomous persons, both the partners and the love relationship can grow, while between dependent partners love often dies of suffocation.

Ecstasy and Despair:

Tennov noted that people in love often interpret their partner's actions as stop or go signals. When they interpret a behavior positively, they feel elation and joy, but when they think they've received a negative message, they feel doubt and despair. It is ironic that the ecstasy and happiness that romantic love brings can only be attained at the cost of increased vulnerability to emotional hurt. In fact, it has been pointed out that only those we love can really subject us to severe emotional damage. Gaylin believes that we can be touched and delighted by an unexpected kindness or courtesy from strangers but when we are "hurt" it is invariably by those we love. Perhaps it is the great vulnerability of partners in love that accounts for the saying that "you only hurt the one you love."

If we could be sure that there was no risk in a love relationship, our vulnerability would be of little or no consequence. Unfortunately, falling in love involves a high degree of risk. For although most people are sure their romantic love relationship will last, the odds are against it. The person we love may take advantage of our feelings and use us. S/he may sincerely love us at first but stop returning our love and later leave us. Or the person may die, causing the greatest pain of all.

This raises the question: Why bother? Why subject ourselves to such hurt and pain? After all, many love relationships are not all that rewarding and may in fact be psychologically damaging as well as emotionally painful.

Nevertheless, most people seem to feel that if they don't take the risk and make themselves vulnerable, they will never really live— that they will have shut themselves off from the most rewarding experience in human existence.

Jealousy vs. Trust:

> *Love is a rose*
> *But you'd better not pick it*
> *It'll only grow when it's on the vine.*
> *Hand full of thorns*
> *And you'll know you've missed it*
> *You'll loose your love when you say the word mine,*
> *mine.*
> *Neil Young.*

We tend to be sensitive to anything we perceive as a threat to our love relationship—anything that could expose us to the risk of being hurt. In this regard, jealousy serves as a legitimate function in alerting us to threats to our relationship—to our security and well being. The more insecure we feel, the more jealous we get.

There are two distinct types of jealousy. The first involves feelings of being left out of some activity in our partner's life—something that takes his/her attention away from us and directs it toward another person or an absorbing interest. We can be jealous of our partner's work or hobbies. A second and more serious kind of jealousy arises from fear of losing love. This may be fear of losing our partner to another person or fear that our partner's love will fade and die. It is not surprising that people with low self-esteem or with experiences of rejection are particularly prone to jealousy. They often tend to perceive threats to their relationships where none exists. And their imaginations may work overtime with agonizing fantasies of betrayal in which they picture their loved ones in the arms of others.

Although it is important to understand the extent to which jealousy can be attributed to past experiences, the ultimate answer to jealousy lies in learning to trust each other. For many people, developing such trust is not easy, since it involves lowering our guard and making ourselves more vulnerable. But trust is essential to the development and continuation of an intimate relationship.

11 ENDING RELATIONSHIPS

"I would say two things. The first thing is that we should separate for a while and the second thing is that we should be friends but not boyfriend and girlfriend. We should be friends but not date personally." Brian.

Landis, a sociologist, estimates that one fourth of all engagements among college students are broken. Causes for breaking engagements include loss of interest, separation, incompatibility, contrast in family backgrounds, influence of family and friends, and various personality difficulties. Of these, loss of interest accounts for most broken engagements. Landis also found that young people usually recover quite quickly from a broken engagement and that the "broken heart" hypothesis has very little foundation in fact. Only 12 per cent of the students he questioned reported emotional involvement lasting more than two years after a broken engagement. Two thirds of his subjects had recovered from the trauma of the broken engagement within six months; fully one third had recovered within one year.

Ideally a breakup should be a mutual decision. Both partners may feel that deeper involvement with each other is not desirable because of life goals, personal habits, or other differences. If so, it is important to share these opinions and the reasons behind them, being careful to minimize hurting one another in the process.

Many times the break up is one sided. One person may want the relationship to end, while the other person wants it to continue. Since a successful relationship requires two willing partners, the one who wants to end the relationship is in a position to make his/her decision to control the situation. Although no situation is ever entirely one-sided, the categories of "Rejecter" and "Rejectee" may help us to consider the different sets of feelings that each party may have in this type of breakup.

In some ways, a rejection is similar to the emotional stages of a divorce.

"I would be sad. I would be sad and boy, I would have a temper. Cause, everybody does that. Boys do that. It's just the opposite of girls. Girls cry and boys have temper tantrums." Brian.

A rejection begins with increasing discomfort in a relationship, which may be shown in being late for dates, conflicts of dates with other activities, forgetting dates, greater frequency and more types of arguments, more hostile comments from one partner about the other's activities or ideas. This then erupts into the actual break, which is immediately followed by surprise or shock on the part of the rejected person. Following shortly after the shock and immediate sadness, feelings of frustration and of anger appear. In coping with these, the recovery period is a time of reorganizing your own goals and achieving a different perspective on your former relationship. This leads to the final stage of re-entry into new or different friendships that may or may not lead to deeper emotional involvement.

The lengths of recovery from being rejected to re-entry is proportional to the depth of involvement in the former relationship, the reserve of emotional strength that you have, and the number of other interests and activities in which you are involved. Typically, one would expect the process to last from approximately two to six months. For this reason, if you were deeply involved with the person who rejected you, you probably should delay any intense emotional involvement or formal plans for marriage with a new partner until at least six months or more after the breakup with the former partner. This will allow you time to stabilize your feelings about your previous partner so that your current relationship is not merely a reaction to an earlier rejection.

If you are rejected by another, analyze the situation carefully over a period of time. Seek to discover to what extent the rejection was due to your behavior, to changes in your partner, and to other situational changes beyond your control. What have you learned about yourself in this process?

What changes can you make in yourself in order to avoid mistakes that occurred in the relationship? Were you too insecure, too controlling, unable to express your feelings, inflexible, disinterested or perhaps bored with your partner? Did you also feel, on some level, that you wanted to end the relationship but were too scared to do so? If yes, explore why you were scared. Examine how far you would have let the relationship go if your partner didn't end it first. Can you turn the rejection to your advantage by seeking to improve your own interpersonal skills and to clarify the type of partner you would enjoy?

If you are involved in a relationship you want to terminate, there are also corresponding reactions you may have. In some ways, the "rejecting" process is similar to the rejected process. There is initial increasing discomfort or disillusionment with the other person, which leads to the actual breakup. After experiencing feelings of relief and guilt, you may also have a period of reorganization and reentry into dating and other activities with other persons.

A person who repeatedly initiates a break up with each of a succession of partners should consider the psychological meaning of this pattern. Some people continually break off a relationship because they fear emotional closeness or intimacy. This is sometimes related to an inability to experience psychological closeness with another, because of painful experiences in one's past, leading to mistrust and fear of rejection. A pattern of repeated instances in which you found it necessary to terminate your relations with various partners may indicate that professional help is needed to aid you in resolving the underlying reasons.

Terminating or withdrawing from a relationship in a constructive manner involves at least two types of skills. One is a "winding down" of emotionally involving activities with the partner. Any activity that formerly meant that you want the relationship to continue should now be discontinued. It is more considerate to do this when you are first relatively certain that you do not want to continue the relationship. Thus you will minimize hurting the other person, rather than implying falsely that you are still "in love" with him or her.

The other skill that is needed is the ability, kindness and courage to share with your partner at least some of the real reasons you have for wanting to end the relationship. In this way, you can assist the other person to become aware of his/her behaviors, values, or habits, that s/he can consider changing. If the other person does not want to change, that is his/her decision, not yours. Nevertheless, you can show your concern by being honest with the other person, so long as you are not brutal, hostile, or overwhelming. As you seek a better relationship with someone else, try to enable the other person to have the same opportunity that you seek.

EXERCISE: Important Past Relationships

Think about your past relationships. Only include those relationships, which were most important to you. List the characteristics that originally attracted you to the person. Do this for each important relationship. List as many characteristics as you can.

_____

_____

_____

_____

_____

_____

When these past relationships ended, what were the specific reasons you told yourself as to why they ended. List each past relationship separately.

_____

_____

_____

_____

_____

How are these reasons (for the ending) related to what attracted you to the person in the first place? Do this for as many different important relationships that you have been in. Try hard to make connections between the reasons you gave for the breakup and what attracted you to the person in the first place. These is a difficult but important exercise so even though it is hard, stick to it and delve deeply into any connection that is a possibility.

_____

_____

_____

A Moral:

A student was kissing his girlfriend good night when they were interrupted by a Japanese student, who proceeded to lecture them on the fragility of love as a basis for marriage. He said in essence, A western marriage is like a hot teakettle on a cold stove. After a while the tea (love) cools. What starts out with a fusillade of fireworks soon gets cold. An oriental marriage is like a cold tea kettle on a hot stove. The basis for the relationship is not blind love but rather a warm friendship—the love grows out of warm understanding, not passionate physical attraction.

12

HOW DO I REENTER THE DATING SCENE?

Once a relationship with one person has ended, do you want to establish dating relationships with other persons? If you "need" or "must" have someone, then you may be seeking a new dependency. If you can live independently without an intense involvement with another person, then you may be ready to consider establishing a new relationship. In this way, you may avoid a "love on the rebound" situation.

To reenter the dating scene, you can tell your friends of your interests, seek activities in which other eligible persons are involved and initiate friendships that may lead to dates and other paired types of activities. Reviewing the reasons for the end of the former relationship may also give you hints on changes you can make in yourself in order to become more attractive to persons in whom you are interested. Sometimes, these changes may even renew a former relationship, turning what seemed to be a permanent break-up into a more constructive interaction with that person.

13 HAVE YOU CONSIDERED IF YOU REALLY WANT TO GET MARRIED?

Why do people want to get married or be in a long-term relationship? When considering mate selection, the first question to ask yourself is, "Do you really want to marry?" To ask yourself the question of whether you want to marry, doesn't have to mean that you are expected to marry although in Western societies, there is a strong norm which pressures persons to marry. Over ninety percent of persons in the United States eventually marry at least once. This, however, does not mean that you must marry. Many people decide that they like the single lifestyle and although there is a tendency in the United States for people to marry, they opt not to.

If you are now single, you may answer, "Yes, I want to marry," or "maybe later", or "never" to the question of whether or not you want to marry. Not every person wants to marry. Especially in contemporary society, with its many lifestyle options, being single does not imply that you are immature, sick, or unable to get married.

Susan was an attractive, young successful TV announcer. She had worked herself up through the ranks and finally held a position she was comfortable with. Although she worked long, hard hours, she loved her job. She had a lovely apartment in Manhattan, which she had decorated in a very sleek, contemporary decor. She loved having friends over for dinner and especially loved inviting friends over for Sunday brunch on her terrace with its magnificent view. She really enjoyed her lifestyle. She came and went as she pleased; her life was full and fun. She had five weeks of vacation a year and loved traveling all over the world. This year she was spending three weeks in Russia and she couldn't wait.

There were men in her life—some more special than others. Although she was not involved in a permanent, monogamous relationship, she dated men whom she had known for years. She felt very close and intimate with several of these men, for she had known them for a very long time. For example, there was John, who she dated on a regular basis. He was someone she met in college over ten years ago. Although she liked him as a friend, and they enjoyed each other sexually, Susan was often secretly glad when he left on Sunday mornings after he had spent the night.

Susan tended to hang out with people who felt the same way as she did about permanent types of relationships and who led similar types of lifestyles. Occasionally she felt pressured to become a "couple," mostly from her parents or her married sister. Her parents felt that she would feel more secure if she married and her sister couldn't understand why she didn't feel the need to have children. Susan felt quite secure in herself and didn't see why being married would add to that security; she also felt that getting married to feel more secure was not a good reason to get married. As far as children, Susan just didn't feel the "urge." Maybe she was too selfish, as her sister suggested," but she didn't want to give up any portion of her lifestyle, which having children would necessitate. She also didn't feel having children was a good reason to get married. And, she secretly felt that her sister was a little envious of her free and easy lifestyle.

Susan was happy, and if her parents and sister would stop reminding her about marriage, she probably wouldn't even think about it.

There are some very positive and constructive reasons that a person may enter marriage, and there are equally good reasons for not marrying. When considering whether or not you wish to marry, it is a good idea to list the pros and cons of each lifestyle as you see them for you. Writing ideas down in a journal helps you to clarify your thoughts.

At the other end of the continuum are those persons who are very anxious to marry, and "dive into marriage." This could be a defense against their anxieties about marriage or against their own negative judgments about being single. Such persons may be ready to marry any person who even faintly expresses interest in marriage. In these cases, the focus is on the couple relationship rather than on the person who one is marrying. This person wants to be married and it almost doesn't matter to whom. An individual who is intensely motivated to seek marriage may be reacting to social pressures, to more basic fears relating to marriage, or to over dependency or rejection in their childhood family. The media also adds to the pressure to marry since the media usually suggests that people marry and "live happily ever after." Some persons may seek marriage as a solution to loneliness or personal inadequacies. A person who has not had the opportunity to discover and examine the daily work of marriage may neglect to balance the fun times with the work times. In other words, even a bed of roses may have thorns.

If you have listed the pros and cons of marriage for you in your journal and feel certain that marriage is what you want, take another look. If your partner feels the same way, ask him/her to look also. Examine in detail what influences are pressuring you both to marry? Look at your parents, other relatives, such as brothers and sisters, and friends. Are they pressuring you to marry? Perhaps they aren't outwardly pressuring you but maybe all your friends have recently married and you may be putting pressure on yourself.

For a variety of reasons, some persons may be absolutely certain that they never want to marry. Some persons have decided against marriage because they have personally had an unpleasant experience with marriage or they have observed an unpleasant relationship between their parents as husband and wife. Some may be overly attached to their parent or childhood family. Some may feel responsible for aging parents. Others may be fearful of failure at marriage and prefer to avoid the possibility of being rejected by a potential partner.

There are also more positive reasons for which persons may decide not to marry. Like Susan in the above vignette, some individuals may commit themselves to a lifestyle or a career that makes marriage difficult or impossible. Others may choose to enter a religious order that does not permit marriage. Some may enjoy the lifestyle of living alone and being able to relocate easily for career or other reasons. A few may have responsibility for an aged parent or invalid relative and decide that marriage would not be possible.

An extreme and absolute "no" to marriage, like an extreme "yes," may mask more underlying reasons for avoiding marriage. Some of these reasons may be unhealthy, while other reasons may be rooted in a healthy commitment to a lifestyle that just doesn't have a place for the work and time that marriage requires. If you quickly say "yes" or "no" to the question, "Do you want to get married," explore your reasons further. Think about the reasons you come up with. Take the opposite viewpoint for a while and then list the pros and cons in your journal.

Many young people plan to marry at some time in life, but may wish to complete other goals such as education, career establishment, saving money, or travel before marrying. For a person at eighteen, "later" may mean several years, but at age twenty-nine, "later" may imply a shorter time span. For many persons, this is an acknowledgment of the gains that can come from the young adult stage of life. For other persons, this delay may result from basic anxieties about marriage.

EXERCISE: Do I Want To Get Married?

Do I want to get married?_____

What are the pros of being married? (List as many as you can)_____

_____

_____

_____

_____

_____

What are the cons of being married? (List as many as you can)_____

_____

_____

_____

_____

_____

What are the pros of being single? (List as many as you can)_____

_____

_____

_____

_____

_____

What are the cons of being single? (List as many as you can)_____

_____

_____

_____

_____

Who in your family wants you to be married the most?_____

_____

What kind of pressures do they put on you to marry?_____

_____

_____

_____

_____

_____

_____

What subtle ways and unsubtle ways do they let you know how they feel?

_____

_____

What other pressures do you feel about getting married?

_____

_____

_____

_____

_____

Who gives you the most pressure to marry?_____

Close your eyes for a moment and in your imagination, your mind's eye, picture the person who gives the most pressure.

What are they saying to you?_____

_____

_____

_____

_____

_____

What do you feel in your body as you are picturing them pressuring you?

_____

_____

Where do you feel the pressure in your body? (stomach, neck, etc.)___

_____

This area then represents your **Pressure Sensitive Area.** You can take care of this area by massaging it, by dancing, and/or by other exercise.

In your mind's eye, what do want this person to say to you instead of the pressure statements?_____

_____

_____

Now put these thought into words. Try to use "I" statements when doing the exercises and try to get in touch with the main feeling you experience such as anger, sadness, joy, happiness.

I want you to tell me _____

_____

_____

because when you say_____

_____

I feel pressured and I feel _____.

14

HOW SHOULD I GO ABOUT LISTING WHAT I WANT IN A POTENTIAL MATE?

"Well right now I would want her to have black hair or blond hair, maybe red hair. It depends on her face. And uh, she would have a nice attitude. Not get mad. Like let's just say I'm a baseball player and I come in the house and I have cleats on and there's just a little dirt on the rug. And she would say, what are you doing and pick that up. I would clean it up whether she yells at me or not." Brian.

"She should have a good job. Cause like say she works in a laundromat and I work at baseball, it's going to be hard for me to pay the salary and the income tax and luxury tax." Brian.

"Well, this is the main part, okay, that I would like her and that she would be cheerful. And that she shouldn't curse." Brian.

Most people have rather definite ideas about what they are looking for in a mate—about what categories of people are "eligible" or "ineligible." They exclude certain potential partners on the basis of such disqualifiers as age, education, race, body type, and social background. The strength of such disqualifiers leads to the screening of dating partners and then potential couple partners to a greater and greater extent.

Of course, people may differ markedly in the characteristics they view as disqualifiers, as well as in the characteristics they are looking for in a mate. A way for you to formulate your ideas about what you want in an "ideal" mate is to make a shopping list. At first it may seem silly, knowing that no such person exists, but keep listing.

Shopping List For A Potential Mate

- Personal Appearance— height, hair, eye color, and so on.
- Personality traits, such as intelligence, dependability, good sense of humor, sensitivity, ability to self-disclose, comfortableness, and so on.
- Economic potential or worth—career potential or attainment, future prospects.
- Attitudes, philosophy, beliefs—basic philosophy of life, values, political leanings, religious beliefs.
- Special interests and abilities—bridge playing, skiing, classical music, or whatever.
- Your secret desires—such as for a fantastic lover.

When you have completed your list, it's time to get down to earth by taking a new page and dividing it into two columns: a must items column and a luxuries column. The "must" items include those characteristics that you consider absolutely essential—that you are unwilling to compromise on. The remaining items on your list become the luxuries—the characteristics you would like to have in a prospective mate but could do without.

As you take this list with you mentally when you go "shopping" for a partner, remember that while it may be possible to change some of another person's characteristics to conform to your must list or even to your luxuries list, it is usually difficult, if not impossible, unless the person understands the changes, considers them desirable, and is motivated to make them. In general, it is <u>extremely</u> unwise to count on being able to change the characteristics of a potential mate who lacks some of your crucial "must" items. In fact, if you have found someone you really care about who doesn't quite meet your qualifications, perhaps you should reevaluate your shopping list.

Make your shopping list as detailed as possible. The process of writing down your "wants" forces you to become more aware of your own needs and desires in a relationship.

EXERCISE: Shopping List For A Potential Mate

List as many characteristics you would ideally like in your potential mate. Don't be modest. This is an idealistic exercise. So, pretend magic happened and you could have whatever mate you would want, what would that person look like?

1. Personal Appearance. List all the specifics, height, weight, hands, etc.

_____

_____

_____

_____

_____

2. Personality Traits. Remember, list as many and be as specific as possible.

_____

_____

_____

_____

_____

3. Economic Potential._____

_____

_____

_____

_____

4. Attitudes and Beliefs._____

_____

_____

_____

_____

_____

5. Special Interests._____

_____

_____

_____

_____

6. Your Most Secret Desires. This is the fun one. Don't leave any out.

_____

_____

_____

_____

_____

Now for the more practical part of the shopping list. Below are two columns. In the left column, list all the "must haves," all the traits that you must have in your potential mate, that you are unwilling to compromise on. The right hand column lists those traits, which you consider to be luxuries, those you will compromise on. List as many traits as you can.

Must Have   Luxuries
(Absolutely Essential)   (Compromisable)

_____   _____

_____   _____

_____   _____

_____   _____

_____   _____

_____   _____

_____   _____

Now look at your present relationship. Are you happy with the amount of "must haves" and "luxuries" you feel you have. Compare your list with your partner's list. Write down your observations.

_____

_____

_____

Translate your thoughts into "I" statements. For example, "I feel I must have more fun in our relationship." Or, "I would like to thank you for helping to create the kind of relationship that is so satisfying to me in so many different ways." Below write three "I" statements that would address three of your "wants" for your relationship.

_____

_____

_____

Once the "I" statements are expressed, you can convey even more specific information to your partner. For example, using the statements that are listed above ... "Three things that I can do to bring more fun into the relationship are ... What would you be willing to do to bring fun into our relationship?" Or, "Some of the ways you help make the relationship satisfying to me are when you bring me a cup of coffee in the morning, when you walk over to me and kiss me for no reason, when you call me in the middle of the day just to say, hi, etc." Below, list specific ways you or your partner can address the "I" statements listed above.

_____

_____

_____

_____

_____

_____

_____

_____

_____

_____

_____

_____

_____

_____

EXERCISE: Traits Of A Potential Mate

If you think about a potential mate, what characteristics come to mind?

_____

_____

_____

What personality traits are the most important to you when you think about a potential mate?_____

_____

_____

_____

What personality traits do you like best about yourself? List them each separately._____

_____

_____

_____

_____

_____

Then take a few minutes and think about all the people that you know who are close to you who bring out the above characteristics. So, if you listed funny above as one of your characteristics in yourself that you liked, think about when you are feeling very funny, who are you with and what characteristics do they have? For example, you may be at your funniest when you're with another funny person or you may be at your funniest when you're with persons who you think have little or no sense of humor.

Your Trait   Other's Trait

_____   _____

_____   _____

_____   _____

_____   _____

_____   _____

_____   _____

Now think about your close friends and/or mates. When you are with them, what personality traits do you think you bring out in them? And how do you do this?

Their Trait   What You Do To Bring It Out

_____   _____

_____   _____

_____   _____

_____   _____

_____   _____

Do you think you bring out negative traits in other people, your mate? If yes, which ones, and what do you do to bring out these traits?

Negative Traits You Bring Out In Others	How You Bring Out These Negative Traits
_____	_____
_____	_____
_____	_____
_____	_____
_____	_____

EXERCISE: Assets And Liabilities

What are your assets (your good points)? Be sure to include as many as you can, physical (pretty, handsome, etc.), psychological (caring, etc.), social (friendly, etc.), economic (good job, etc.).

_____   _____

_____   _____

_____   _____

_____   _____

_____   _____

What would your mate say are your assets?

_____   _____

_____   _____

_____   _____

_____   _____

What traits in yourself would you like to work on, improve?

_____   _____

_____   _____

_____   _____

_____   _____

_____   _____

What would your mate say you need to work on, improve?

_____   _____

_____   _____

_____   _____

_____   _____

_____   _____

What are your mate's assets?

_____   _____

_____   _____

_____   _____

_____   _____

_____   _____

What would you say your mate needs to work on, improve?

_____   _____

_____   _____

_____   _____

_____   _____

_____   _____

What would your mate list as his/her assets?

_____   _____

_____   _____

_____   _____

_____   _____

_____   _____

What would your mate list as his/her traits needing improvement?

_____   _____

_____   _____

_____   _____

_____   _____

_____   _____

Now, if you can, compare lists with your mate and discuss the potential for growth you have with each other.

15

HOW DO YOU GO ABOUT FINDING A PARTNER?

"I would look in, uh, Orlando, Florida, the Bahamas, Hawaii — in all the sunny places. Like islands and stuff. Cause there's a lot of girls on the beach. I'll pick one up." Brian.

Although we tend to glamorize the mate selection process in our society, some social theorists believe that mate selection takes place in what can be called a "marriage market." The merchandise consists of eligible men and women who can be exchanged for a given price. The currency used in the marriage market consists of the socially valued characteristics of the persons involved, such as age, physical appearance, and economic status. In our free choice system of mate selection, we typically try to get as much in return for our social attributes as we can. To settle for less would be a bad exchange.

While we in the USA tend not to think of the marriage process in this way, this market orientation to mate selection is much more apparent in societies where marriage is arranged by the parents. Since the merchandise bears a price tag, the task of the parents is to find a suitable match among families of roughly equivalent social status. Of course, when a dowry — money, goods, or property brought into the marriage by the bride— is involved, the parents may try to marry their daughter into a family of higher social status. Such an exchange of money or property for higher social status is considered a good deal by both families.

Social exchanges are not guaranteed to be equitable. People in an inequitable relationship feel uneasy. People who find themselves in this situation usually try to convince themselves and others that the relationship really is equitable. If they fail at this attempt, they are likely to terminate the relationship. A possible exception is the person with low self-esteem and a negative self-concept. Whereas persons with high self-esteem tend to choose their mates, those with low self-esteem tend to underestimate their own social attributes and settle for a mate.

Inequity in a relationship may also result from changes over time. Social attributes that are important in one generation may become outmoded or irrelevant in the next. And it is important to note that the qualities that initially attract one person to another — their virtues— may later lose their appeal and become vices. In either case, the person would not marry the same partner given the opportunity to do so over again but would instead look for a new mate with more modern attributes or better virtues.

Tina is a very pretty 23-year-old graduate student. She has devoted much of her time and energy to her studies and after she finishes her Masters Degree wants to continue on to get her Doctorate in Psychology. Although she had a boyfriend when she was an undergraduate, she hasn't had a steady boyfriend in about three years. She is very popular, has a lot of friends, and goes out quite often. But, even though she's surrounded by her friends, and leads a busy enjoyable life, she feels she's missing that "special person." It isn't that she's interested in getting married; she doesn't see that happening for quite some time. She just wants to have a steady partner with whom she can go out on a fairly regular basis.

The problem is that she doesn't know how to go about finding that special person. At this point in her graduate career, the classes are much smaller than they were when she was an undergraduate so there aren't that many people in her classes. And the ones who are generally much older. When she goes out with her friends, they usually go to a movie or out dancing. She doesn't ever meet anyone in the movies and when she goes out dancing, there aren't that many guys she sees who are attractive to her. Often after they all go out, Tina gets depressed because it seems to her that she'll be alone forever. She just doesn't know how to go about meeting a nice guy.

How do people go about finding and identifying the "perfect" mate for them? Many factors are involved, including opportunities for interaction, similarity and complementarity of backgrounds and interests, and various "market" costs and rewards. Keep in mind though that success in marriage is much more than finding the right person; it is also a matter of being the right person.

The impersonal isolation of modern life makes it particularly difficult for many people, especially in large cities, to meet eligible mates. While there seems to be millions of people in our society, single people often question, how do you meet people and get acquainted? And how do you increase your chances of finding someone who is right for you?

If you want to find someone to love and marry, two researchers by the name of Walster and Walster recommend that you associate with a variety of eligible persons on a fairly regular basis. They consider it unfortunate that so many unmarried Americans subscribe to the myth that one's true love will somehow happen along if they just sit and wait. And people are so often reluctant to admit that they are searching for a mate—and even if they would admit to it, they usually don't know how to undertake such a search. But the Walsters conclude that if you are going to find eligible partners, it is necessary to get involved in social activities— a little theatre group, a ski club, a crafts class—something in which you are already personally interested. In short, make a point of exposing yourself to a wide range of interesting people rather than pinning all your hopes on one person. And maintain exposure on a regular basis, since people tend to respond more positively as they get to know each other. Most people end up with someone they see on a day-to-day basis, a factor called differential association.

A social scientist did a study to examine how people met each other. He asked 1800 individuals and found that only 22% fell into the category of couple pick-ups. Very few of these pickups had occurred in singles bars or similar places designed for romantic encounters. All of the pick-ups had been unplanned and had happened in such diverse places as buses, restaurants, stores, and even elevators. More than 40% of the sample had met their partners at college or at work, while 13% had grown up with their future partners. They had married the boy or girl next door. Interestingly enough, couples who had met in college, at work, or in that magical chance encounter had approximately equal divorce rates- all high- whereas the 13 % who had married the girl or boy next door showed the lowest divorce rates.

One relatively recent innovation in meeting people and matchmaking is the use of videotapes as a go-between. Here it is possible to view the tapes of people who seem to fit the qualifications that you are looking for in a mate, and the ones you are interested in are invited to view your tape. If one of them returns your interest, names and phone numbers are exchanged and you take it from there.

There are also innovations in computer dating. In the absence of face-to-face contacts, for example, businesspersons in various parts of the country are now able to hold conferences by means of computer terminals. It does not seem farfetched then that persons who are found to be compatible by computer matches— including those living in different parts of the country or even in different countries— could interact by means of computers, perhaps leading to in-person interactions.

The general idea of computer dating services (Match or JDate) and other types of introduction services (speed dating) such as by mail is that each participant answers a series of questions about his/her background, beliefs, interests, and related personal information. Sometimes, questions will be combined to form an assessment scale of some type. Each person's answers are then placed on a card or tape file and compared to all other persons in that file. A "match" consists of locating persons in the file who answered the same set of questions in the same way. Sometimes, an index of similarity is calculated in an attempt to make the procedure "objective" or "scientific." The usual assumption is that maximum similarity (not optimum similarity) is desirable.

> *Adrienne was an attractive, intelligent woman in her early forties. She was divorced for over thirteen years. Her two sons were eighteen and nineteen, and this September, the younger one was leaving for college. The older boy, already in college, was entering his sophomore year. Now after all these years, Adrienne would be alone. She looked upon this time with ambivalent feelings. On the one hand, it might be lonely and she knew she would miss her boys. They were so much a part of her life.*

On the other hand, her time would be her own for the first time since they were born. She was looking forward to this and planned to take courses toward a second Masters Degree, something she had wanted for a while. She also looked forward to no more kitchen mess, no more arguments between the boys, no more dirty laundry all over the bathroom and all the other small annoyances that are part of parenthood.

Adrienne dated occasionally. Earlier she had been involved in a rather unpleasant long-term relationship, which had finally ended. Since then, she had dated several persons but no one had really sparked her interest. That was the one part of her life that she was sad about. She wanted to be in a relationship with someone special—someone with whom she could share her life. But that didn't seem to be happening, so she involved herself in her work and the boys.

This summer, after the boys left for college, she decided to go visit her sister in Texas for a week. On her way home, her plane was delayed and she had to wait four hours at the airport in Dallas. While waiting, she began talking with a man who was also waiting. They hit it off. She liked him a lot and for the first time in a long time, she felt excited about the possibility of a relationship. Ray was a teacher (so was she) who was flying into New York and then driving up to Montreal where he lived. As it turned out, when they reached New York, they decided to spend a week together in Manhattan to get to know each other better. They had a good time. Since then, they have maintained contact by phone, through letters, and once a month they fly to one another (taking turns). Adrienne is taking a sabbatical next year and thinking about finding a temporary teaching job in Montreal to see if she would like living there. Ray is also very excited about this possibility and wants Adrienne to move in with him.

It is important to note, though, that computer and mail introduction services are only as good as: (1) the types of questions each person answers; (2) the size (larger the better) of the file that the computer service has; (3) the honesty and motivations of the participants who respond; (4) the extent to which a paper and pencil questionnaire is representative of one's real life behavior; and (5) the research and theory underlying the whole procedure.

No one but no one knows the exact factors involved in happy matches. And even if we did, we still are faced with the difficulty of measuring these reliably. If you are seriously considering a computer matching service, investigate the company, find out how it matches persons and what type of persons apply, and consider whether you have better alternate opportunities to meet persons in face to face situations. The best you can expect from computer matching (or introductions by mail) is to find names of persons you might not have found otherwise. Whether they have serious interests in marriage, or even in desirable companionship, can only be determined through your personal contacts with them.

Such computer contacts could make the person's search broader, and it would serve to minimize embarrassing face-to-face rejections. However, people who have used computer-dating services often feel that the computer matchmaking is unable to capture the biochemical spark that seems to occur in more spontaneous meetings. Thus, the old concept of proximity still operates in the sense that eventually two people have to meet, interact, and fall in love before deciding to marry.

> *Joanne, a 37-year-old banker, wanted to meet someone with whom she could have a serious relationship. She was having a hard time finding someone. She felt that the guys she met in the discos were jerks, "only interested in one thing." All the men at work were married. And the rest of the men seemed to be gay. After several years of "looking," she decided to try a computer dating service. Before she answered any questions, she made lists and lists of exactly what she wanted in a mate. She spent hours deciding if she wanted someone who was outgoing or reserved; whether sense of humor was more important to her than dependability. Finally after months of searching inside herself trying to discover what it was that she wanted in a mate, she handed in her answers.*

A few weeks later she received a call from the agency. The woman said they had found exactly the right person for her. Joanne met him and it was true, he did have exactly those qualities that she had listed as important. They dated several times, and Joanne tried to like him. She liked him, but she didn't LIKE him. Something was missing. She never did quite figure out what it was. Eventually, she stopped seeing him.

Even though researchers and computers seem to be able to pick out "perfect matches" for people, that "spark" that people mention seems to be the important criterion. It is unlikely that researchers or computer programmers will be able to identify exactly what each person's "spark" is composed of.

Stephanie was an attractive, never married, thirty seven year old woman. She was a professor at a small community college. She loved her job; it gave her plenty of free time in which she ran a consultation service for women, running group seminars on how to succeed as a woman in business. Throughout the years, Stephanie had many boyfriends but for one reason or other, they never seemed to work out. Stephanie had been depressed for a couple of years after her father had died, and during that time had not felt like dating anyone. Afterward, there just didn't seem to be anyone interesting around. Her friend suggested that she write an ad in the personal column of the newspaper. She had heard of someone who met the person they eventually married through the personals.

Stephanie was reluctant but after spending two months sitting at home with no prospects for a date, wrote an ad, and sent it in. Shortly thereafter, she received over fifty answers to her ad. She and her friend spent an entire Saturday afternoon and evening squealing in laughter as they read some of the replies. Even so, there were some who sounded interesting. She called and set up dates with a few of the men. While a few of the men were interesting, none of them worked out—either they weren't interested in her or she wasn't interested in them.

> *A few months later Stephanie went to the florist to buy a floral arrangement for her friend's birthday and started talking to the owner of the shop. They started dating and now, three months later, they are talking about marriage.*

The success of commercial introduction services still depends heavily upon the clientele they attract. Usually a person with average initiative and social competence can be just as successful in finding datable persons ion other ways.

EXERCISE: What About Your Interests?

List all the different interests that you have_____

_____

_____

_____

_____

_____

What places do you go to explore these interests?_____

_____

_____

_____

_____

What interests would you like to explore but haven't had time to explore?

_____

_____

_____

What is the one thing you could do next week to increase your exploration of one of your interests?_____

_____

_____

And what could you do the following week?_____

_____

_____

16

WHAT ARE SOME FACTORS ASSOCIATED WITH FINDING A MATE?

As early as 1859, O.S. Fowler saw nature as like marrying like: "Do lions naturally associate with sheep, or wolves with fowls, or elephants with tigers?" If you love pistachio nuts, why settle for walnuts?

Social Class

> *Jeanie, a 36-year-old graphic arts designer, met Ted, a 34-year-old manager, at a singles bar. She seemed to really like him, which was unusual for the people she tended to meet at these places. In addition to liking him, she was physically attracted to him. They began a relationship and at first were quite happy. Initially, they tended to isolate themselves from other people because they wanted to spend most of their time alone in order to get to know each other better. They seemed to have similar energy levels and liked doing active things, like riding bikes and playing tennis. He was a good athlete and she was also.*

Just to give you some ideas about what we do know about mate selection, researchers know that certain general factors operate as far as people meeting and marrying. They are social class, geographic location, intelligence, age, race, ethnic group, religion, physical appearance, education, previous couple status, values, and role compatibility.

Social class reflects occupation, income, and education but residence, language, and values. It reflects an entire life style. One researcher found that men and women from high status homes where the father was a professional or a marginal professional were most likely to marry those who had fathers in the same occupational level. The same was true of the middle grouping of business, secretarial, and minor government occupations, as well as for the lowest grouping of skilled, unskilled, or farming occupations.

As time went on, though, Jeanie started to notice "things." For example, while he told her he was a manager, it was a food store that he managed. And, when they went to a movie and discussed it afterward, it seemed like they saw two different movies. He just didn't see her "hifalootin" point of view. Sometimes when she would speak about issues, she felt his way of looking at things was too different from hers. He didn't know about the typical college experience (primarily because he didn't go to college, as she later learned). When she started introducing him to her friends, he didn't seem to fit in. While at first her friends tried talking to him about various things they all were interested in, they soon gave up because he didn't seem to know or be interested in what they were talking about. They, in turn, were not interested in his primary interest, sports. The icing on the cake came when she brought him to meet her parents. At dinner, he didn't know which utensils to use nor did he know the names of some of the foods he was eating. She was embarrassed for him. He also was very uncomfortable and the tension level between the two of them was high. On the way home, they argued and he called her a snob.

Their relationship ended after a heated argument. At times, Jeanne missed Ted. She often felt guilty about the possibility of her being a "snob," but she knew it could never work out between them. They were just too different.

Social class determinants in mate selection are mainly the occupation, income, area of residence, and education of the couple and their parents. Mate selection is limited by social class in two significant ways. In the first place, since a person associates mainly with people in the same social class, s/he is more likely to meet a prospective mate from within his/her class than outside it. In addition, since speech patterns, dress, educational level, interests, and even jokes vary considerably from class to class; the person is usually more comfortable, self-assured, and compatible with a potential mate from his/her own social class.

Geographic Closeness

The theory of geographic closeness states that the probability that A and B will marry each other decreases as the distance between their residences increases. One study found that half of the residents who were married in Columbus, Ohio had actually lived within sixteen blocks of each other at the time of their first date.

Donna, a 28-year-old nurse, met Bob, a 29-year-old physician's assistant on a ski weekend. They hit it off right away and began to date. Dating, however, was a problem since they lived eight hours away from each other. At first they saw each other every weekend. Bob would drive down to see Donna on Friday night. He would get to her apartment about 3 A.M. He would sleep all Saturday morning. Saturday evening they would go out and Sunday morning he would start his long trek home. When he got home, he then would have to prepare for the week ahead. He often started Monday morning off exhausted. After a while, they spread out their dates to every other weekend. At times, they were so exhausted from their jobs and their commuting every weekend that they would even go every three weeks before seeing each other. Eventually, their relationship started to fizzle. Bob met someone else at work that lived in his area and it just seemed so much easier to date this new woman than to travel eight hours to see Donna.

Donna used to tell him that if he really loved her, he wouldn't mind the trip. Sometimes he thought that maybe she was right but he just couldn't handle the exhaustion.

Where you live can be merely another reflection of social class membership, but in our highly mobile and rather casually class-structured society, geographic location can work in mate selection as a factor that is independent of or overcomes social class differences. For example, most people in our society attend public schools, which are generally highly mixed in the social classes represented (although area of residence could be based on social class so that the public school would contain persons from the same neighborhoods).

Similarly, many communities and neighborhoods, particularly in and around urban centers contain persons from all social-class levels except perhaps the very highest and the very lowest.

Traditionally, geographic closeness was a stronger factor operating in meeting and marrying. That is, people were most likely to marry the boy or girl next door— or at least someone in the same neighborhood or at the same school. In today's highly mobile society, however, this principle is more applicable to small communities than to large cities.

That we can only marry those with whom we interact is obvious. But there is a more subtle meaning to the propinquity theory of mate selection. We tend to date and marry those with whom it is convenient to interact. Being in the same class, or working at the same job, or living a few blocks from each other permits convenient interaction.

Intelligence

Joanie, a 33-year-old high school history teacher, was dating Ronnie, a 37-year-old construction worker. She met him one summer at the beach and was immediately taken with his good looks and strong, tanned, body. She was immediately physically attracted to his blonde hair and blue eyes, which twinkled when he squinted into the sun. They seemed to get along okay and enjoyed doing a lot of the same activities, like going out for dinner and having picnics in the park. They also loved the beach in the summer and enjoyed sailing together. The problem occurred mainly in the winter when Joanie wanted to go to the theatre and then discuss the music or the play. Ronnie hated the theatre and hated classical music as well.

> *While Joanie wanted to discuss the meaning of the play, Ronnie wanted to watch the football game. Once he fell asleep during the ballet, snoring loudly until Joanie kicked him. Joanie loved to explore philosophical questions and when she tried to communicate her feelings about the meaning of life, Ronnie asked her what her problem was, "You're born, you work, and then you die. That's it. There's nothin more. Why are you makin things so complicated?" When they argued, she felt like they weren't communicating. She would tell him that she felt like she was loosing her identity in the relationship because she couldn't talk to him about anything that was important to her. He would answer, "Here's money, go buy a new dress, you'll feel better." After six months, their relationship ended. They still see each other occasionally but only on a friendly basis.*

Intelligence acts as a factor for homogamy because two people of different intellectual ability usually cannot communicate easily with each other, even though a close relationship may be present in other dimensions such as physical attraction, mutual interests, friends, etc. Without a similarity of intelligence, the relationship will end unless one of them is uniquely attractive to the other in terms of some other significant status attribute. Going steady, courtship, and marriage require intensive communication; the identification that takes place at each stage of a developing relationship is not only physical and emotional but intellectual as well. If there is a wide difference between intelligence levels, this identification will almost certainly fail to occur.

Age

> *Bob, a successful 54-year-old businessman, met Regina when she was 23. Regina, home from college for the summer was waitressing at the country club where Bob was a member. Bob, always a flirt, fooled around with Regina, never thinking that she would make anything out of it, especially since she knew Fran, Bob's wife of 30 years. Regina sought Bob out every time he was at the club and soon Bob started seeing her outside the club. He began having an affair with her, which lasted for about a year before he told his wife. He told Fran that he believed that he was in love with Regina and wanted to continue seeing her. He moved out of his house, got an apartment, and pursued his relationship with Regina.*
>
> *Regina's parents were up in arms when they learned of this relationship and started calling Bob a pervert. They tried to bribe Regina so that she would stop seeing him. They continued to see each other. Eventually Bob decided that the relationship with Regina could never work because of their age difference and he ended it. Regina continued to call him, stating her love for him but Bob stood firm and refused to see her. He said he felt he had to try to work on his marriage because it was only fair for Fran. He started dating Fran, trying to make the relationship work. He missed Regina terribly and tried very hard to put her out of his mind. He knew in the long run she would be better off and he felt that he owed it to Fran to work on the marriage. If he could have his druthers, if the world were a different place, if age didn't matter in this society, Bob knows he would be with Regina but he felt it could never be.*

In our own society, it is usually considered appropriate for a younger woman to exchange her youth and beauty for the financial security and higher social status of an older man. However, it has been considered inappropriate for an older woman of high economic and social status to marry a much younger man. With increasing equality of the sexes, however, this pattern may gain greater social acceptance.

Thus there are social pressures that appear to restrict your couple choices to certain groups and geographical factors, which influence you to choose those with whom it is convenient to interact. In addition to the other factors, homogamous factors also operate. The homogamy theory of mate selection states that you are attracted to and become involved with those who are similar to you in age, physical appearance, education, social class, and couple status. In other words, "like marries like."

Mate selection in our society usually occurs between two persons about the same age, although the man is almost always slightly older than the woman. The median age at which American men first marry is 23.1; for females, it is 21.1. College attendance delays the age of marriage by a year or two so that the most frequent age of marriage for college graduates is 22 for women and 25 for men.

The tendency for males to marry down and females to marry up in age, social class, and education is referred to as the mating gradient. Such pairing results in some high status women and low status men remaining single. Recently women are achieving higher education levels, getting better jobs and making good salaries in today's society. Many of these high status women report that the pool of eligible men is slim and unless they are willing to "settle," which many are not, they opt to remain single. A few have chosen to have a child out of wedlock in order that they might have a "family." As a function of the mating gradient, though, the upper class woman will receive approval from her parents and peers only if she marries someone of equal status. On the other hand, approval is usually not withheld from the male who marries below himself in age and status.

The older the groom in our society, the greater the age spread between the man and woman, although the respective ages of the couple still remain fairly close. The highly publicized marriages between men in their sixties and seventies and women in their early twenties are in reality statistically insignificant.

Race

> *Don and Marianne met at the university where Don was a doctoral candidate and Marianne was a social work student. They started dating and fell in love. They both found each other to be intelligent; they came from similar middle class backgrounds; they enjoyed being together; they loved making love. Their relationship developed over the next two years and they started talking about marriage. They decided they would marry after Don defended his doctoral dissertation and graduated. They knew it was time to tell their parents. Unfortunately, their parents were completely against the marriage because Don was black and Marianne was white. Marianne thought her mother was going to have a heart attack because she suffered from high blood pressure. Marianne's father told Marianne that he would do anything for her if she would stop seeing Don. It was a terrible time for both of them. Although they felt their love was strong, they loved their parents and families also and didn't want everyone to be so upset. Their friends were supportive but the daily phone calls from their parents were driving them crazy. They had a long talk and decided to elope and get it over with. They were sad that they couldn't have a simple nice wedding celebration with their families present.*
>
> *They had a rough time at first. People would look at them when they walked through the mall hand in hand, but they got used to it. Don got a job teaching at the university and Marianne started work at a social service agency. Now five years later, they are still happy. They have two children, a boy and girl. They own their own small home and they like their jobs. Their families settled down after the children were born and race is no longer an issue for them. Their parents can now understand why they married each other. Don and Marianne still sometimes feel funny when they go on vacations or even outside the university community because people stare at them and their children. But they still feel they made a good decision.*

Race is an obvious factor in mate selection. Interracial marriages rarely occur in our society and accounts for only 1 percent of all marriage in our society.

The highest rate of interracial marriage occurs with servicemen stationed overseas. The world wars, the Korean War, the war in Vietnam, and the continued stationing of American men in many parts of the world have meant a slight increase in interracial marriages. Interracial marriages also take place occasionally on college campuses, where students from many different nationalities and racial and ethnic groups are brought together without the customary patterns of parental supervision and without the usually provincial and prejudiced environment and pressures of the home community.

Largely because of social pressure, interracial couples that live in this country face problems that intraracial couples do not encounter in other places. Probably for this reason there is a statistically higher rate of marriage failure, and a lower birth rate, among interracial couples than among intraracial couples.

Ethnic Group

An ethnic group is a sub society that shares the same cuisine, language, dress, religious observance, and, to some extent, recreational interests and is embedded in a larger and ethnically distinct society. Ethnic characteristics, when they do not also include a racial distinctness from the major portion of the society, are not often socially restrictive on mate selection. Most ethnic groups intermarry widely with the majority population and with each other. The mass media and the public school system in our culture have virtually eliminated significant ethnic differences within a generation or two

Dolores and Tony met in high school. He was a tall, dark haired Italian with incredible blue eyes. She was Irish—a small pretty red head with perfect white teeth and big dimples. As soon as he saw her, he told his friend that she was the girl he was going to marry. He walked over to her, and started talking to her but although she thought he was very attractive, she thought that he had been with every girl in creation. He persisted and she eventually said she would go out with him. They started to date and she learned that he wasn't always the big tough guy—that there was a soft, affectionate, caring, loving side to him. Although their parents had always wanted them to marry "someone of your own kind," they eventually reluctantly accepted them as a couple. Dolores and Tony married during their second year in college and have been married now for fifteen years.

Most ethnic groups are more like other groups in their particular geographic location and social level than they are unlike them. Consequently information about a person's residence and educational level usually reveals more about his cultural pattern than does information about his ethnic group. If any ethnic characteristics restrict interethnic marriage, it is most likely to be differences in religious observance.

Religion

Barbara and Larry married each other when they were both twenty-seven. She was a Roman Catholic and he was Protestant. Neither one, however, was very religious. So they thought there would be no problem in their marriage around religion. Two years after they were married, Jason was born. At first there was no discussion about religion but then Barbara told Larry that she had been thinking about having Jason baptized Catholic. Larry said that he thought they were going to raise their children non-religiously and then when the children were older, they could decide for themselves. Barbara told him that she felt that way before the baby was born but that now that the baby was actually here, she felt differently. They began to fight more frequently about whether their child should be baptized in a Catholic Church or not and the discussions soon became quite heated. Eventually they entered marriage counseling over this issue.

Mary and Steven were married in a double ceremony performed by a rabbi and a priest. Neither one was raised in a very religious home and neither practiced. Relatives voiced concern over their marriage because of their religious differences but they were in love and believed that it wouldn't be a problem. And it wasn't. They celebrated everything—both Jewish and Catholic. They actually became more religious in the process— in both religions. They celebrated Easter and Passover, Christmas and Chanuka. As each holiday passed, they each explained the traditions behind the holiday. They looked forward to each holiday and enjoyed them thoroughly.

Religion used to be among the most significant of the forces for homogamy. Traditionally, of all marriages in the three major religions in the United States, less than one in ten was interfaith. Now, however, as strict adherence to religions of all types declines, many more interfaith marriages are occurring.

Physical Appearance

Janine was an attractive young woman of twenty-four. She was studying for her Masters Degree in Elementary Education. She occasionally dated but there was no one special in her life. One day while she was waiting on line to register for classes, she met Bo, a graduate art student. Since the line to register was so long, they had quite a bit of time to talk. After they registered, they continued their discussions over soda. This led to dating. Janine liked Bo, a lot. She felt he was intelligent and fun to be with. But she didn't find him physically attractive. When he went to kiss her goodnight on the lips, she turned her head. She just couldn't help it. She just didn't find him physically attractive.

Having further narrowed your potential couple partners to those of similar age, you will be influenced by the way they look. Studies indicate that people tend to become involved with those who are similar to them in physical attractiveness.

Education

Paula and Mike were married when she was eighteen and he was twenty-one. Mike was a police officer and shortly after they were married they bought a small house in the suburbs. There, for the next fifteen years, they raised two sons. When the boys were in high school, Paula, who had been a housewife up until this point, decided to go to college, something she had always wanted to do. She enrolled in a local community college, taking two courses. She loved school; it was stimulating and exciting and she began to meet all new people. At first Mike was supportive of Paula's decision to return to school. He felt it would keep her busy.

After a while, though, he started to feel it was keeping her too busy! And he didn't like her new friends. They seemed snobby.

When she would get excited about someone new she met at school, he would seem disinterested. When she became excited about a new idea that was discussed in class, he would say it was boring. She began to feel that he wasn't interested in her school and they began to argue about it. At one point, when she was studying for an important exam, he screamed at her, "where are my socks?" And then they proceeded to argue about this for hours. Not only was she late for her exam, but also she was nervous and upset while taking it. She was furious with him. He wouldn't admit that he didn't like the school idea nor would he discuss it with her. As time went on, Paula started to spend more and more time away from home with her new friends.

In addition to age and physical appearance, the level of education you attain will influence your selection of a mate. If you've gone to college, you are likely to marry someone who has gone to college. In general, there is a strong tendency among both men and women to marry someone who is within one educational level (up or down) to them.

But there is more to being attracted to those with whom we share something and those we enjoy. The approval of others affects our initiating and continuing a relationship.

Previous Couple Status
There is a tendency for the divorced to marry the divorced, the widowed to marry the widowed, and the never married to marry the never married.

Values
In addition to living nearby and being like each other in terms of personal and social characteristics, whether or not two people become involved with each other may be a function of holding similar values. We are less drawn toward people who look like us, sound like us, or share our mannerisms than we are toward people who agree with us. Someone who agrees with us validates our self-confidence. When the person we date shares our values, it confirms that they approve of us and enjoy being with us. We feel like congratulating them on their ability to know quality when they see it. But, while couples that share values may enjoy each other, it is not clear whether their shared values are the cause or the result of their interaction.

Role Compatibility
Before increasing your commitment to someone who shares your values, you are likely to become concerned about role compatibility. Both you and your partner will take two sets of role expectations into marriage, those you will act out and those you will expect your partner to act out. Whether or not you expect to cook, do laundry, or sleep late on Sunday mornings, will depend in large part on your observation of your parents and of other husbands and wives. While your primary models have been your parents, the role behaviors of your married brothers and sisters and friends will also influence the roles in your marriage.

Who does what in any given marriage is not important. Agreement on role responsibilities is important.

Conclusions:
So what can we conclude from examining the research? We can conclude that marriages are most likely to occur between people of similar social class, who live near each other, intelligence, age, race, ethnic group, physical appearance, education, and couple status. Researchers do not agree on the extent to which people select as couple partners others with similar personal and social characteristics. However, the researchers do tend to agree that holding similar values is one of the most important variables.

Thus, various sociological factors help to account for your attraction to and involvement with potential couple partners. While living nearby implies that you will only become involved with those with whom it is convenient to be involved, other factors involve an element of choice. But social pressures tend to limit choices to those of similar age, physical appearance, education, social class, and previous couple status. After these influences have been felt, you will tend to focus on the values and role expectations of your potential partner. But initiating and continuing your relationship will also depend on psychological factors.

Because of greater social mobility in our society, as well as the lessening of parental influence and the changing cultural norms, young people are finding greater freedom to marry across racial, ethnic, religious, and social class lines, and such marriages are likely to become more frequent in the years ahead. In general though differences in race, ethnic background, social class, and religion— as well as in such characteristics as sex-role expectations, interests, and values—add to the problems that the couple partners are likely to encounter. In a major survey done by sociologists Tavris and Jayaratne, the conclusion was, one lesson this survey shows is that like should marry like. Ultimately, of course, the outcome depends on the persons involved.

EXERCISE: Same Or Different

Take a few moments to think about your past relationships. Then, think about age, race, religion, ethnicity, education, social class, common interests, values, goals, and any other factors you can come up with.

Which factors, in general, do you pick in your relationships? For example, do you pick someone who in general is of the same race and education level as you but much older? Make a list like the one below for each important relationship that you've been in. What are the general patterns you can learn about yourself and your relationship choices?

Factor	Same As Me	Different
Age	_____	_____
Social Class	_____	_____
Education Level	_____	_____
Ethnicity	_____	_____
Race	_____	_____
Religion	_____	_____
Values	_____	_____
Interests	_____	_____
Intelligence	_____	_____
Common Goals	_____	_____

What patterns have you learned from doing this exercise? _____

_____

_____

_____

_____

17 DO OPPOSITES ATTRACT?

> *Billy and Jill met each other at a party given by a mutual friend. He was dark, tall, good-looking and rather quiet. Jill was a small, elfish-looking blonde who was the life of the party. Billy was attracted to her "positive energy." She was attracted to his "quiet strength." Both were very attracted to each other, quickly began dating, and married after only five months. After marriage, they learned that the differences between them were even more pervasive. She liked classical music; he liked jazz, which she hated. He liked sports and would spend hours watching television; she liked riding her bike and being outdoors. She wanted to talk about their relationship; he would sit silently, waiting for her to stop. After a few years, his silent strength was redefined by Jill as cold and not willing to talk about his feelings. Billy redefined her positive energy as mania.*

There are two old sayings about coupling: "Birds of a feather flock together," and "Opposites attract." While both of these sayings have elements of truth, both have been amplified by modern observations.

As we stated in the last section, it has been assumed that the most significant factor in mate selection is the similarity of the two people involved. People are attracted to, become involved with, and marry those who are similar to them in age, race, religion, social class, and other characteristics. Common interests, beliefs, goals, and values are also conducive to the development of a close relationship that can, in turn, lead to marriage.

The term for the idea that opposites attract is complementarity. This concept essentially refers to a couple's having complementary needs— needs that fit together. To put in more bluntly, each person makes up for the other's deficiencies. Sociologist Robert Winch believes that within the field of eligibles, persons whose need patterns provide mutual gratification will tend to choose each other as marriage partners. For example, a person with a strong need to dominate would be gratified by and tend to choose a submissive partner.

This situation described above is very typical in that couples frequently redefine what initially attracted them to each other as negative. In this sense the seeds of conflict are contained within the relationship from its earliest beginning.

It is most useful for couples that are planning to marry to list all the qualities that first attracted them to each other. For it is these very same qualities, which they may well argue about at some later point. For example, the wife who is caring later may be described by her husband as intrusive. The husband who initially made her feel safe and protective later is experienced as overprotective and smothering. If couples can take their lists of the qualities that initially attracted them and translate them into negative words, they can foresee areas of potential conflict and hopefully discuss ways of working through these issues.

Persons with different characteristics, drives, or needs sometimes select one another as mates, with attraction being based on complementary factors rather than on similar ones. In other words, within the field of eligibles— some people (most) select mates in terms of similarity factors such as similar age, intelligence, and social class, etc. In other cases, mate selection is influenced by the complementation (or oppositeness) of certain specific personality traits or needs.

Do complementary needs explain why a person will be initially attracted to one another? Probably not. Initial attraction is probably based on similarities, on factors of shared interests, values, and backgrounds.

Complementary needs are significant mainly in reinforcing and perpetuating the relation after it has been initiated. If these complementary needs are not satisfied in a relationship—even though the factors of shared interests and background and romantic attraction are present,—the relationship may be discontinued. The complementary needs that seem to be the most forceful in a couple relation are dominance-submission, nurturance-dependence, vicarious-achievement, and hostility abasement.

A person who needs to be dominant in personal relations usually will regard a relatively submissive companion as compliant and agreeable; the submissive person, in turn, will look upon the dominant one as dependable and decisive. On the other hand, two equally dominant people may consider each other bossy, opinionated, and competitive and they may enter into power struggles with each other. Thus, in terms of this dimension, people with opposing needs may be drawn together in mutual satisfaction, and people with similar needs may be driven apart or have constant clashes. Two primarily dominant people, for instance, if they have somehow been drawn into a marriage, may engage in a perpetual cold war- vying with each other for dominance, unconsciously attempting to undermine each other, and eventually involving children and other family members in an unending and stressful power struggle.

In our society, although changing, the male is still expected to be the dominant partner, providing for and protecting the female and children. However, it is becoming increasingly acceptable for the female to play the dominant role. Of course, a person may be dominant in one area and submissive in another area. The wife may be dominant in making decisions concerned where the family should live; the husband may be dominant in choosing which car to buy. Usually, however, each person demonstrates a characteristic dominance or submissiveness in most matters, as a reflection of his/her total personality structure; and in most relationships, whether friendship or marriage, reciprocal role interaction will not occur unless there is a relative balance of dominance and submission, so that each is able to relate to the other in this regard in ways that are mutually satisfactory.

A nurturing person derives satisfaction primarily in giving sympathy, emotional support, and aid; a dependent person derives satisfaction primarily in receiving sympathy, emotional support, and aid. Although everyone is both nurturing and dependent to some extent, in any relation one person usually will be characteristically nurturing most of the time, and the other will be characteristically dependent.

With regard to the dimension of achievement, some persons have a strong need, or capacity, to derive vicarious satisfactions from the achievements of another. In contrast, some people have high achievement needs. The person who obtains satisfaction from identifying with another and vicariously experiencing his/her triumphs can form a complementary relation with a person who is achievement oriented. If both people are achievement oriented, there may be rivalry and competition. Similarly, if they are both high on the dimension of vicariousness, there will be little in the other for each to identify with.

One final example of a trait, which may be complementary, is that of hostility-abasement. If one person demonstrates a relatively high hostility need in relation to another's relatively high abasement need, the two persons will be able to form a satisfactory interaction, at least in this one dimension. As we will discuss in a later section, one of the common categories of marriage is the conflict-habituated marriage in which the relation actually depends on a continuing series of conflicts. This type of relation is illustrated in Edward Albee's play Who's Afraid of Virginia Wolf? Or typified by the Mae West song, "You're So Mean To Me." In the play, the need of the dependent husband to be abased is matched by the need of the dominant wife to be hostile, although these needs were sometimes interchanged. The couple interaction is thus one of mutual role reciprocation, with equivalence of need satisfaction on the part of both partners.

In some marriages, which are later to become problemed, often there is an increasing polarization of roles where one will only be "allowed" to be dominant, for example, and the other will only be "allowed" to be submissive. The rigidity of such relationships is likely to create severe hostility and resentment, with each person feeling locked into a rigid role definition. Flexibility in relationships is perhaps as important as any other relationship factor we've discussed thus far. Relationships need to flip-flop, with one taking the dominant role sometimes and then taking the submissive role at another time. In this way, there is more complexity in the relationship, with each person nurturing as well as being nurtured.

Although a couple may differ in ways that tend to complement each other's weaknesses, they are not usually "opposite" in the sense of being markedly different in interests, beliefs, goals, and values. In short, complementarity does not necessarily mean dissimilarity in important or crucial characteristics. But although complementarity in needs could be important in mate selection, similarity appears to be more important.

Also, while it seems at first glance that like marrying like and opposites attracting are contradictory terms, they are really manifestations of different levels of interacting. Like marries like relates to the real shared components in a relationship such as common interests, common relationship goals, common intellectual pursuits and further serves as a sustaining element in a healthy relationship. Opposites attracting, on the other hand, could occur in two ways. The first is where there is a conscious appreciation and respect for the other's differences. However, in some cases, persons are operating at a fundamentally unconscious level where one person feels that they are missing certain qualities that the other person possesses. This raises the unconscious fantasy that they will join with the other person emotionally so that they can become a complete human being. They feel that they can borrow some of the qualities from the other person. This then creates for them a sense of longing and excitement about the other person, which they tend to define as love.

Now that we know the roles that similarity, and complementarity play in couple selection, can we use this information to predict whether two people will appeal to each other as marriage partners? Or can we use this information to predict whether the marriage will last? Unfortunately there is no way that we can predict the occurrence of that biochemical spark of physical attraction. In the presence of sexual chemistry, that psychological "click," whether one is similar or different to another is likely to be irrelevant. Furthermore, we are unable to predict how two people will get along or fit in terms of personality makeup. When two people seem to have everything going for them but somehow lack such personality "fit," the situation is called interactive disqualification. Admittedly Cupid's arrow does not strike at random, but we still cannot predict where and when it will strike. Romantic love and mate selection remain intriguing mysteries—as they perhaps they should be.

EXERCISE: Do You Match?

This exercise will help you determine if you feel that you and your potential mate match each other in terms of similar amounts of assets and liabilities. List your assets and liabilities in the left hand column and in the right hand column list your mate's assets and liabilities. Next to each asset (under "score"), place a number ranging from 1 to 5, with five representing a very important asset. Next to each liability, place a -1 to -5, with -5 representing a very bad liability. Next add up all your assets, add up all your liabilities. Subtract your liabilities from your assets. This is your total score. Do the same for your mate. See if you match.

Your Assets	Your Liabilities	Mate's Assets	Mate's Liabilities
_____	_____	_____	_____
_____	_____	_____	_____
_____	_____	_____	_____
_____	_____	_____	_____
_____	_____	_____	_____
_____	_____	_____	_____

TOTAL Scores

Your Asset Score _____ - Your Liability Score _____ (=Your Total)

Mate's Asset Score _____ - Your Mate's Liability Score _____ (=Mate's Total)

Your Total _____ Mate's Total _____

18 WHAT ABOUT EXPECTATIONS?

"I would be nice. I would clean up. I would buy her things, and myself things. I would be friendly to her. I would be a friendly person." Brian.

Expectations are those behaviors that you want or would predict as being the most likely or most desirable in a certain situation. Expectations come from many sources. Some expectations refer to yourself. You may expect to have a particular type of job, live in a certain area, make a certain amount of money etc. You also have a set of expectations about your mate. S/he will also have images of you. It is crucially important to try to flush out what your conscious and unconscious expectations are for yourself, your partner, and your relationship.

A good match is not a matter of being similar or opposite on a particular point. What is important is whether the two partners agree on their expectations that they should be similar or different in certain ways. For example, one couple may feel that both partners should spend much time together, so they do spend much time together and judge their marriage as being very happy. An unsuccessful couple, on the other hand, may have one partner who expects to have a lot of separate or individual time. Whether they spend much time together or have a lot of separate activities, they are likely to judge their marriage as less successful because of their underlying conflict about what they "should" do as a couple. Still another couple may agree that each partner should have a lot of time apart from the other- they actually do have a lot of separate activities, and they feel they have a very successful marriage. It is the matching of actual behavior to expected behavior that results in one's judgments of the success of the relationship.

Part of the matching process consists of exploring as fully as possible whether the two persons approach life tasks in similar ways. When differences exist, then it is important to see if the two persons could work out a mutually agreeable pattern that both genuinely accept? This is very possible if both have similar values and respect for each other. Mutual general agreement on both content and process adds up to compatible lifestyles, including healthy ways of resolving differences when they occur, as they inevitably will.

19

HOW DO YOU ACCOUNT FOR MATE SELECTION ON A PSYCHOLOGICAL LEVEL?

THE ROLE OF INDIVIDUAL DYNAMICS IN COUPLE PROCESSES

Here's A Knot Called Jill

> *I don't respect myself*
> *I can't respect anyone who respects me*
> *I can only respect someone who does not respect me*
> *I respect Jack because he does not respect me*
> *(From Knots by R.D. Laing)*

How Come A Person Could Have All The Right Social Variables And They Don't "Connect" And Then Sometimes They Could Have All The Wrong Social Variables And Then They Do?

In the earlier sections, we discussed how social variables are usually the first filter through which we choose our mate. Next psychological variables come into play. In the course of his or her unique history within a particular family environment a person passes through many stages of development. Each stage in turn is characterized by distinct yet changing relationship phases. One must learn to be close without becoming emotionally fused with others, how to be independent without being disengaged, how to separate from the family of origin without becoming emotionally cutoff, and how to dissolve old relationships and form new ones without projecting the old into the new. The life cycle confronts everyone with the task of mastering these different phases of interpersonal relating.

The fully mature person who has completely mastered these many phases, however, stands as an ideal on a continuum of interpersonal competency. Such a person would be able to participate in a wide spectrum of relationship phases, all the while remaining objective and comfortable with the level of emotionality appropriate to each. This individual could give care and nurture to others, where fitting, without becoming overinvolved and over responsible for them. S/he could also receive the care and support of others without becoming unduly enmeshed or dependent on them. Such a person would be capable of self-initiated action and self-reliance without becoming estranged and disengaged from other, and would be able to allow others the same independence and individuality. This fully functioning person could maintain his or her own boundaries of selfhood while respecting the integrity of others. S/he would not transgress the boundaries of others, nor would this person fall short of responsible involvement with them. A repertoire of interpersonal competency would have been built up over the life cycle of such a person, enabling him or her to maintain the delicate balance between individuality and mutuality in close human interaction. Sounds wonderful, doesn't it? However this is an ideal, rather than a reality.

Many relationship theorists believe that most persons bring to marriage gradations of incompleteness with respect to these developmental tasks in human interaction. One partner coming from a history of overinvolved or enmeshed family relationships may not know how to appropriately separate and be independent. Coming from a family environment marked by disengaged or alienated relationships; another partner may not know how to be comfortably and suitably close and supportive. Growing up in a family where children were not valued, another mate may have learned to deny, distort, or conceal elements of his or her selfhood. Deposits of lingering resentment and disappointment are often laid down in the personality of such a person. In the quest for individuality another partner may be locked into an extreme sense of isolation from his or her family of origin, with the emotional cutoff that accompanies this position. Another's partner's life may have been filled with times of deprivation or exploitation in the family of origin, laying down an enduring sense of imbalance in relationships. This person carries into marriage a chronic sense of relationship deprivation, on the one hand or, of being intruded upon, on the other. For yet another partner, times of relationship dissolution, such as death or divorce, may remain emotionally unresolved, with enduring emotional fixations around such feelings as grief and sadness. For another partner, estranged from certain members of the original family, feelings of forgiveness and acts of rejoining remain blocked.

Marriage then, presents mates with new and most critical life tasks. Ways must be found for responding appropriately to the partner in the present, for continuing the resolution of unfinished relationship tasks from the past, and for mastering the never-ceasing challenges and vicissitudes that inexorably arise in the course of marriage. In relationship formation several dynamics occur at once. There is, on the one hand, a tendency on the part of each partner to repeat and to continue interaction models observed and experienced in the family of origin. Partners openly and secretly seek to replicate relationship patterns experienced in that field of interaction, for at least they are familiar. On the other hand, each partner hopes to enrich his or her original developmental environment, to have what was not present and available in that childhood environment. This unconscious longing to vary one's earlier history lays the basis for an intuited, implicit hope for completing unresolved relationship tasks. Partners then seek to complete unresolved relationship tasks. They then seek in their mates the kind of interaction that will enable them to correct, to master, or to gain restitution for unfinished business from the past.

Most theorists believe that the matching process in relationship formation is uncannily accurate and complementary. Coming into the relationship with their individual expectancy sets, partly conscious and partly unconscious, partners intuitively find in the partner certain objective traits and characteristics that meet their respective subjective needs. The mate whose history was grounded in a disengaged family model strives for a sense of involvement with the other, for overt and covert levels of closeness and support. The mate whose history has been lived out in an enmeshed field of relationships seeks overt and covert levels of personal freedom and autonomy, thus establishing a basis for a clearer differentiation of self. The mate who is emotionally cutoff from his or her family of origin unconsciously seeks in the partner one who is still deeply involved in an extended family with the belonging that families affords. The partner whose prior experience has been one with a great deal of exploitation or deprivation may seek out that mate with whom his or her undiminished disappointments or resentments can be repeated and redressed. Because we all strive for wholeness, the unexpressed hope is that the partner can help to complete or at least complement one's own unresolved relationship tasks and impasses.

In its earliest origins, then, the intimate relationship is comprised of complex and interlocking systems of intrapersonal and interpersonal forces. Individual expectancy sets and needs have to be met through interactional patterns that are mutually satisfying and balanced. Partners can relate to each other adaptively, by recognizing and preserving their separate identities. But they can also relate with varying degrees of maladaptive interaction, in which past patterns are displaced onto the present, where they are out of context and inappropriate. The emerging relationship then becomes characterized by the symbolic reenactment and reconstruction of earlier unresolved and uncompleted interactions. The new partner is then covertly maneuvered into being an overinvolved, disengaged, critical, deceased parent, or other important personage from past times.

We can observe that in unresolved couple conflict there is an equivalence of personality structures. Both partners display similar basic problems in relationships, but they tend to play them out through contrasting roles. Similarly conflicted partners encourage each other's problematic behavior and develop an unconscious arrangement of collusion. They both do this even though in choosing this particular partner they had unconsciously intended to become whole—to come to terms with their existing problems. Thus the couple conflicts originate in similar basic personalities in both partners. Both partners tend to have comparable experiences with regard to the marriages of their parents and, as a result, have a similarly colored image of their own social, psychological, and sexual role as well as that of their partner. This is called collusion. Collusion refers to an unconscious agreement of two or more persons, which is concealed from both of them, and which is based on similar unresolved conflicts.

This common unresolved conflict is acted out through different roles, which gives one the impression that each partner is the exact opposite of the other, when in reality they are the flip side of the same coin. The bond of the similar, core conflict causes one partner to seek their wholeness through progressive escalation of their behavior and the other through de-escalation behavior. This escalation behavior on the part of one and de-escalation behavior on the part of the other is a major reason for the mutual attraction and the resulting bond. Each hopes that the other will release them from their core conflict. Both believe themselves now to be protected against the things they fear most and expect that their needs will be met more than ever before. In the long run this collusive attempt to solve the problem fails because the repressed elements in both partners return. So that what once was transferred onto the partner (projected and externalized) reemerges in one's self.

The basic idea of thus far is that we select mates who are more or less our equals. When we are on a search-and-find mission for a partner, we size each other up as coolly as business executives contemplating a merger, noting each other's physical appeal, financial status, and social rank, as well as various personality traits such as kindness, creativity and a sense of humor. With computer-like speed, we tally up each other's scores, and if the numbers are roughly equivalent, the trading bell rings and the bidding begins. As stated earlier, it appears that each one of us is compulsively searching for a mate with a very particular set of positive and negative personality traits, a composite picture of those traits that represent the positive and negative traits of our early caretakers. The unconscious mind plays an enormous part in mate selection. Everything that was still is. Today, tomorrow, and yesterday still exist all at the same time. Understanding this basic fact about the nature of your unconscious may help you understand why you sometimes have feelings within your relationship that seem alarmingly out of proportion to the events that trigger them.

You fell in love with your partner because your unconscious believed you had finally found the ideal candidate to make up for the psychological and emotional hurt you experienced in childhood. Our unconscious self contains the storehouse of inner childhood needs, our unfulfilled desire to be nurtured and protected and allowed to proceed unhindered along a path to maturity. Socialization imposes other demands on us. Each society has a unique collection of practices, beliefs, laws, and values that children need to absorb. Mothers and fathers are the main conduits through which these norms are transmitted. This indoctrination process occurs in every family in every society. There seems to be a universal understanding that, unless limits are placed on the individual, the individual becomes a danger to the group. But even though our parents often had our best interests at heart, the overall message handed down to us was a chilling one. There were certain thoughts and feelings we could not have, certain natural behaviors that we had to extinguish, and certain talents and aptitudes we had to deny. In thousands of ways, both subtly and overtly, our parents gave us a message that they approved of only a part of us. To fill the void, we create a false self, a character structure that serves a double purpose: it covers up parts of us that we feel need to be hidden and protects us from further hurts. At some point in life, however, this form of self-protection becomes the cause of further hurt when we are criticized for having these negative traits. This occurs when others condemn us for being distant or needy or self-centered or fat or stingy. Our attackers do not see the hurt and vulnerability we are trying to protect, and they do not appreciate the clever nature of our defense.

So that as adults, we are a composite of our lost self, those parts of our being that we had to repress because of the demands of society, our false self, the facade that we created in order to fill the void created by this repression and by a lack of adequate nurturing, our disowned self, the negative parts of our false self that were met with disapproval and therefore felt we had to be deny. So the only part of this complex collage that we are routinely aware of is the parts of our original being that are still intact and certain aspects of our false self. Together these elements formed our personality, the way we would describe ourselves to others. Our lost self is almost totally outside our awareness; we severed nearly all connections with these repressed parts of our being. Our disowned self, the negative parts of our false self, hover just below our level of awareness and is constantly threatening to emerge. To keep it hidden we have to deny it actively or project it onto others. "I am not self-centered." Or, "You're so lazy."

EXERCISE: Your Family Legacy

Below is a diagram including three generations. Position yourself in the genogram, the older generation being your parents and finally, the oldest, your grandparents.

List all the important factors such as age, age at and reason for death, divorce, alcoholism, mental illness, drug usage, abortion, etc. Fill in as many factors in the genogram as you can. Try to include personality characteristics as well.

Try to explore the legacy your family gave you.

In your family, what did you learn about being a man/woman?_____

_____

_____

_____

_____

In your family, what did you learn about the opposite sex?_____

_____

_____

_____

_____

In your family, what did you learn about relationships, marriage?___

_____

_____

_____

_____

In your family, what did you learn about sexuality?_____

_____

_____

_____

_____

_____

Try to list as many learnings as you possibly can. It will help you be more aware of what processes you were handed from earlier generations.

EXERCISE: More On Early Caretakers

The following exercises are meant to help you understand how your early relationships affect your present day relationships.

Try to remember when you were just a small child living in your childhood home. What do you remember about that home._____

_____

_____

_____

What else do you remember?_____

_____

_____

Picture your room, the place where you slept. What do you remember about your room, your bed_____

_____

_____

Can you remember your Mom in that home? What feelings do you have around her when you were a little child?_____

_____

_____

Can you remember Dad in that home? What feelings do you have around Dad when you were a little child?_____

_____

_____

Were there any other significant caretakers in your life while you were a small child? What special feelings do you have around them?____

_____

_____

Still thinking about your childhood home, list the most positive personality traits of all your significant caretakers as you were a young child growing up.

_____

_____

_____

_____

_____

List the most negative traits of all your significant caretakers as you were growing up._____

_____

_____

_____

_____

_____

Circle the three most important positive and negative traits of your early caretakers.

The positive traits you circled are probably those aspects you listed earlier as qualities you most liked in your potential mates.

The negative qualities you circled are probably those aspects you listed earlier as reasons why your relationships ended.

Still picturing yourself in your childhood home, please complete the following:

What I remember most about my father is (List as many different things as you remember)

_____

_____

_____

What I wanted most from my father and didn't get was_____

_____

_____

_____

_____

The most important thing I wanted from my father and never got was

_____

_____

Some of the things I did in order to get _____from my father were

_____

_____

_____

What I remember most about my mother is_____

_____

_____

_____

What I wanted most from my mother and didn't get was_____

_____

_____

_____

The most important thing I wanted from my mother and never got was

_____

_____

_____

As a child, some of the things I did when I didn't get from my mother
were _____

_____

_____

These exercises teach us about our areas of sensitivities. If love was
what we wanted from our father, and if we didn't feel like we got love
from him, as a child we did all sorts of things in order to get love. In
our present relationships we may complain about feeling unloved
by our partner, because that is our area of sensitivity. We probably
do the same things we did as young children in order to get the love
from our partner.

Thinking about the exercises, can you see any of your areas of
sensitivities that have carried over from childhood? List as many as
you can.

_____   _____

_____   _____

_____   _____

_____   _____

_____   _____

_____   _____

_____   _____

_____   _____

List the behaviors that you do in your present relationship in order to get these areas of sensitivities soothed.

Area of Sensitivity   What You Do To Get Soothed

_____   _____

_____   _____

_____   _____

_____   _____

_____   _____

When your partner doesn't soothe you, you feel just like you did when you were a little child when you didn't get what you wanted from your mom or dad. The hurt is just as great. You will do the same behaviors that you did as a child now in you present relationship in order to get what your partner is not giving you. List as many of these behaviors as you can. Try to list the brattiest things that you say, do to your partner in order to get what you need

_____

_____

_____

_____

_____

_____

_____

Before we leave childhood, can you complete the following?

The best gifts (psychological) my father gave me were_____

_____

_____

_____

_____

The best gifts my mother gave me were_____

_____

_____

_____

_____

In your mind's eye, picture yourself with your dad in your childhood home; Picture yourself as a child in that home. Picture yourself as a child in your childhood home looking at your Dad. Can you see him as a human being struggling in his own relationships—doing the best he knows how? Can you forgive him for not giving you what you wanted from him as a child, for not being your perfect Dad? I forgive you, Dad. Can you walk over to him and thank him for the gifts he did give you? Thank you, Dad. Can you give him a hug? I love you, Dad.

In your mind's eye, picture yourself with your dad in your childhood home; Picture yourself as a child in that home. Picture yourself as a child in your childhood home looking at your Mom. Can you see her as a human being struggling in her own relationships—doing the best she knows how? Can you forgive your Mom for not giving you what you wanted from her as a child, for not being your perfect Mom? I forgive you, Mom. Can you walk over to her and thank her for the gifts she did give you? Thank you, Mom. Can you give her a hug? I love you, Mom.

Now imagine just you in your childhood home. Imagine yourself when you were just a little child. Imagine yourself in your favorite room in your home that you grew up in. Picture some of the details about that room—the windows, the furniture. See yourself in that room. Please complete the following about yourself

Looking at myself as a child in my mind's eye ...

I feel_____

_____

The scariest part about looking at myself is_____

_____

_____

The best part about looking at myself is_____

_____

_____

Now, in your mind's eye, walk over to the little child who is you and tell her the three most important things that you want him/her to know

1. _____

_____

2. _____

_____

3. _____

_____

Now tell the little child who is you that you love him/her, give him/
her a hug if you like, and saying good-bye, walk away.

Below, write down what you learned from this exercise.

_____

_____

_____

_____

_____

_____

_____

_____

_____

_____

_____

_____

_____

_____

_____

20

IS LOVE A SOUND BASIS FOR MARRIAGE?

People do not agree as to whether love is a sound basis for marriage. One study found that sixty five engaged men and women defined love as companionship, understanding, sharing, and giving of mutual support. It could be that marrying for love would be conducive to couple unhappiness. People would become dissatisfied with marriage because it does not provide the close companionship that they married for. These students were asking more for marriage than it could deliver. This is significant because these participants tended to have a realistic attitude toward love and a realistic view of love has traditionally been thought of as a good preparation for marriage.

When romantic love is considered, most writers and researchers issue glaring indictments against it as a basis for marriage. Writer Duvall states that romance is poor preparation for marriage and is not to be trusted to provide more than a few thrills. It is not enough to marry. Researcher De Rougemont states that of all the possible motives for marriage such as equal social level or education, suitability of temperament, background, religious preference, age etc., love is the most unstable and ephemeral and yet is heralded as the most important motive.

One marriage and family counselor noted that the qualities that make a man or woman comforting and fulfilling as a marriage partner have little direct connection with the qualities that usually arouse feelings of romance. For example, an attractive glamorous man or woman may or may not also be a dependable, growing, caring person.

In contrast to this negative view of romantic love, sociologist Spanier studied 218 married college students and found no indication that romantic love, as opposed to realistic love, was harmful to couple adjustment.

What about romantic love and happiness in your marriage? If the love you have for your partner is based on physical attraction, little time together, and few shared experiences, marrying on this basis may be taking an unnecessary risk. To marry someone without spending a great deal of time with him/her (minimum of one year) in a variety of situations (your home, your partner's home, in many different social situations etc.) is like buying a Christmas package without knowing what's in it. We need to spend time studying our partner.

Many people flinch when they hear the word study or analyze in reference to their love partner. However, individuals who get divorced spend a great deal of time analyzing their relationship with their partner, trying to discover what went wrong. It is better to study our partner and our love relationships <u>before</u> considering marriage.

There is some evidence that the love myth is dying (love is all we need for a successful marriage) and being replaced by a non-jealous, non-possessive love. One explanation seems to be that because more people are living together, they are learning more about the opposite sex. Having to deal with grocery shopping, meal preparation, dirty dishes, laundry, stomach viruses, and clothes on the floor, provides a more realistic setting in which to explore each other.

In marriage there is usually a fairly constant interplay of altruistic, companionate, sexual, and romantic love. The relative importance of these four components will, of course, vary for any given couple, with altruism or companionship or sex or romance being more prominent in some marriages than in others. The relative importance of these four components also varies for any couple with the duration of their marriage. In the very early stages of marriage, for example, the sexual and romantic components are generally predominant.

Obviously, the most significant influence on the relative prominence of one or another of the components of married love is the immediate love need of one or both of the persons in the relationship. The love needs of a person will vary from time to time in a marriage, and these needs will not always coincide with the needs of the other person. But the societal expectation is that each will fulfill the particular need of his/her partner, not because s/he shares that particular need at that particular time but because s/he recognizes the need in the other. S/he provides the need as a love offering. On occasion such provision will be simultaneous and mutual but more often it is alternate.

As long as in the long run, there is a balance of at least the alternate form of love fulfillment in marriage; as long as a person feels that s/he is getting as much as s/he is giving and that the partner is giving because s/he wants to rather than because s/he feels s/he must, the marriage should be happy and fulfilling.

Despite the mass media emphasis on sex and romance, the companionate side of love—shared dependence, mutual respect, and "belonging"— probably has more to do with what the average couple experiences as conjugal love than does the passionate romantic attachment of Romeo and Juliet. We must remember that part of the essence of romantic attachment of Romeo and Juliet was its brevity. The modern Romeo and Juliet did not have to go to work and expend most of their time and energy performing all the various routine, mundane, and nonromantic activities necessary to meet the obligation of supporting their family. Their couple relation may have continued to include the passion and idealism of the romantic sexual love of their youth- at least on occasion- but an increasingly important factor in their relationship would have been the satisfactions of shared responsibilities and experiences in meeting the practical demands of daily circumstance, in providing support and companionship to one another, and in loving and launching their children. These satisfactions would not only assume an added importance but might even come to constitute the chief basis of their relation.

21

WHAT DO THE MARRIAGE THEORISTS THINK ABOUT SELECTION PROCESSES?

Basically, the marriage theorists have adopted a very different theory of mate selection process. While the theorists that were discussed earlier focus on individual selection factors (why A chose B), the couple theorists address the process of how and why A and B choose each other as a joint decision. Unlike the positions stated earlier, these theorists examine the interpersonal process of mate selection. This unspoken process has been referred to as "collusion," "family projection process," "pseudo-identification," "trading of disassociations," or "merging." These theorists suggest that an unconscious contract exists where each partner chooses the other and enters into an agreement to fulfill the other's needs.

They believe that individuals choose partners who have similar concepts of the meaning of a relationship. Driven by a desire to form an interpersonal union, individuals choose each other as partners in such a way that their own habits, feelings and ideals are confirmed. The formation of this union is structured by the concept of collusion which encompasses the ideas that partners are joined on the basis of similar kinds of unresolved conflicts around which an unadmitted and hidden game occurs. It is in this interplay or cooperation that the partners take on roles, which create an impression that they are, characteristically, opposites of each other. But, in actuality, they are "polarized variants of the same conflict."

Marriage counselors Nicols and Everett state, "The process of selecting a mate is not magical or mystical but an expression of each individual's personal needs and development in a particular socio-cultural context. They feel that individuals choose partners based on their own previous relationships with parents in their early lives.

Family therapist Ackerman stated, "Particularly significant is the disguised motivational element of searching out a mate who is likely to assuage or counteract one's personal anxiety ... It is often said that one neurotic marries another ... It is common knowledge that the neurotic tendency of one couple partner often complements that of the other ... When one partner exhibits pathological anxiety responses, the other usually does too (p.165)." He believed that mate selection as being based on unconscious signals or cues by which partners recognize the other's "fitness" for joint working through or repeating of still unresolved splits or conflicts inside each other's persons- at the same time sensing the guarantee that with that person, they (conflicts) will not be worked through.

What this means is that each partner unconsciously attempts to maneuver the other into some earlier relationship pattern in their family of origin: each has a disquieting feeling that some old tormenting ghost has risen to haunt him. Of course, the partner must cooperate to complete the process needed to maintain the relationship.

Relationship counselor Virginia Satir discussed some of the effects of previous relationships on an individual's choice of a partner. She believes that, "Without necessarily knowing it, parents are the architects of their children's romantic and sexual selves. I believe that two people are first interested in each other because of their sense of sameness, but they remain interested over the years because of their ability to enjoy differences. Another family therapist, Carl Whitaker, states, "If you assume that the beginning of the marriage is a transference phenomenon, then the choice of a couple partner is infinitely accurate: It's unconscious to the unconscious (Neill and Knistern, 1982, p. 173)." According to Whitaker, mate selection is "done with the same kind of exactness that you would expect of a computer." The combination of a husband and a wife is an extremely accurate one.

Scharf states that although the choice of the couple partner often seems to have been made very quickly, on the basis of little conscious knowledge, it turns out with great accuracy of complementarity and facts of personalities and even life experiences of the partners. Couples quite often turn out to have striking similarities in terms of childhood experiences. The marriage partner is a person who connects us to parts of our beings, which are completely suppressed, lost to memory, and yet well remembered at an almost cellular level.

Marriage counselor Napier, who gives considerable emphasis to the process of mate selection states, "If there is any single principle in our selection of mates, it is in my view that we marry someone who is a kind of psychological twin. We are all indeed in search of someone who will help us feel psychologically complete. We are attracted to someone whose basic psychological situation in his/her family of origin is similar to our own. That is, we identify with this person's core problems, dynamics that were shaped in the early family.

Imago therapist Hendrix and the object relations theorists discussed in an earlier section believe that in psychological development from infant to adult, a part of ourselves is repressed. He calls this the "lost self," the part that is repressed due to its unacceptability. As individuals reach maturity they seek to fill emptiness inside themselves caused by this repressed side of the personality. As a result, individuals seek mates whose personalities are complementary to their own. They have a template, "Imago," of what they long for in a partner, which in reality is the composite of all their impressions of their original caretakers. When individuals find someone who matches this imago, they become intensely excited because their unconscious believes that this relationship will provide the nurturing they have been longing for and in this manner they will regain their original wholeness.

What these therapists believe over and over again is that not only does like marry like with regard to the social and psychological variables; but that individuals who marry have selected each other on the basis of psychological completeness— that they are psychological twins of each other. What this means is that couples enter into agreements (unconscious) with each other and that they cooperate with each other to maintain whatever patterns are existing in the relationship.

In this sense it is useful to think of couples as being one united mass and to speak in terms of we. So that if a couple has a particular problem, let's say one of them has an affair, it would be helpful, although probably not too palatable, for the couple to examine the affair in terms of "weness." "Because of our childhood histories we have tremendous fears of intimacy, so that when we married, we unconsciously agreed to do whatever was necessary to remain at a certain safe distance from each other. When and if anything happens that serves to reduce (bring us closer) the distance between us, one of us will do something to bring the distance back." This is the unconscious contract a particular couple could have. When couples examine their relationship in this way, it then becomes useless to blame, criticize, or attack the other for any behavior that s/he may be doing. Instead, the couple needs to do the safe environment exercises to work the issue through. If the issue is a serious one, the couple should seek professional help.

22 HOW CAN YOU REALLY "KNOW" THIS PERSON IS THE "RIGHT ONE" BEFORE THE WEDDING?

"Well, I would stay with her for about ... This is my point of view. I would stay with her for about ten months and see what she says and I would ask her to marry me. If she says no, I'll wait two more months and make her really happy and then I'll ask her again." Brian.

"I would just sense it. If we really liked each other and we both really knew it and if we both knew that we liked each other, I would stay with her. If we <u>really</u> liked each other and it was like eight months, two months earlier than the ten months, I would make an exception." Brian.

There is no absolutely certain way you can predict how you and your mate will interact in the future. But the best predictor of future behavior is past behavior. This is a little difficult to apply to a love relationship, however, because there is always the possibility that one or both partners are concealing completely from the other person certain expectations or personality characteristics. There is no way to "try" marriage, just as there is no way to try being age sixteen before you actually are that age.

The matching process, however, is neither blind nor due simply to chance. There are ways to make approximate predictions of what it will be like to be marrying, matching, or living with another person before you actually do it.

Some Suggestions:

- Be with your partner in the same situation on many occasions. In this way you can discover whether s/he is consistent and acts the same way under similar circumstances.
- Be with your partner in a wide variety of situations, and especially experience times together when you are under stress or pressure. Stressful times tend to allow the other person to respond most real, with less opportunity to maintain one's best appearance. Unexpected situations also provide opportunity to observe how your partner reacts when s/he fails to get his/her way, is not in complete command of the situation, or must adjust to a new or

unfamiliar circumstance. Stressful times tend to bring out other aspects of a person's personality that they would tend not to reveal in calmer situations. These unexpected situations also provide the opportunity to observe how your partner meets and deals with situations when they cannot be in control or cannot have their way. Here considerations of flexibility, reaching out for help, being honest about limitations and accepting their difficulties play an important role.

- Observe the lifestyles of the people who are close to your partner, such as his/her parents, siblings, friends, or others. It is quite likely that a person will have developed response patterns that "fit" the lifestyles of those who are closest to him/her. It is probable that each of you will use your typical interactive patterns in relating to each other.

- Watch how you resolve conflicts. At some point or another, you will clash. This will result in conflict. Conflict is healthy. Don't panic. It's impossible to spend any amount of time with a person and not have different opinions about an issue or not get on each other's nerves. It is not that there is conflict in a relationship that is the problem—all relationships have conflict—the more important question is, how does the conflict get resolved? Does the conflict get resolved or are you still arguing about the same issue that you argued about six months ago.

- Does your mate nurture you? Or, are you doing all the nurturing in the relationship? While, in some couples, one will nurture and the other will be nurtured, it is important that both be able to take both these roles. Many situations will arise during a lifetime that will require both of you to be able to support and nurture each other.

It takes time to see each other in a wide variety of situations on many occasions and to observe how relatives and friends of each partner typically live and interact. At a minimum, at least one year of rather intensive association is advisable, since this permits you to move through one annual cycle of holidays, birthdays, and seasonal activities. It doesn't matter what you call this experience (friendship, engagement, etc.) but it greatly matters that you allow sufficient time to gather reliable data about how you relate to a potential mate. Compared to the anticipated length of your marriage (fifty years?) allowing a year to explore the many variables involved is well worth the increased probability of success.

23 WHAT FACTORS CONTRIBUTE TO COUPLE SUCCESS?

Observers by no means agree on the reasons for marriage and failure and consequently do not pretend to make infallible predictions of couple success even before a couple is married. Despite disagreements about the causes of marriage failure, certain factors contributing to the success of marriage can be isolated. These contributing factors are childhood background, age at marriage, vocational preparedness, emotional maturity, present interests, length of engagement, and adequate sex education. In addition to these factors, which are discussed below, the homogamous and heterogamous factors discussed earlier (race, ethnic group, social class, etc.) all correlate with couple success.

Childhood Background
Most studies since 1937 have agreed that a person's background is the single most important factor determining couple success. Specifically, the person most likely to have a successful marriage has the following background:

Factors Related To Couple Success

√	Parents who are happy in their marriage.
√	A happy childhood.
√	Lack of conflict with the mother.
√	Home discipline that was firm but not harsh.
√	Strong attachment to the mother.
√	Strong attachment to the father.
√	Lack of conflict with the mother.
√	Parental frankness about sex.
√	Infrequency and mildness of childhood punishment.
√	Attitude toward sex that is anticipatory and free from disgust or aversion.

In contrast, a person whose parents were unhappily married and who was him/herself unhappy as a child is unlikely, statistically speaking, to make a successful marriage. In other words, couple happiness, as well as couple unhappiness seems to run in families.

Age at Marriage

Most studies agree that youthful marriages (before age twenty) are much less stable than marriages that occur after this age. There are several possible interpretations of why these earlier marriages are less stable than later marriages. Personality changes occur with the passage of time. New interests emerge and new skills develop. The mate a person would choose in adolescence might not be the one s/he would choose at age twenty; and the one s/he would choose at age twenty might not be the one s/he would choose at age twenty-five; or again at age thirty. In general, however, s/he is better equipped to make such a choice in his twenties than in his/her teens. The person in his/her teens usually has not had the experience of being an independent adult, whereas the person in his/her twenties usually has acquired some concept of him/herself, is aware of his/her chief values and is generally better equipped to choose a mate.

Moreover, early marriages occur most frequently in lower class families and the relative instability may simply reflect the socio-economic pressures of this group. Third, if the husband or the wife does continue his/her education while the other person works, the one continuing to study in this way is likely to outgrow the other, acquiring a subculture of a higher stratum and coming to feel that the other has lowbrow tastes or is intellectually inferior.

Finally, in many young marriages, the wife is pregnant before the marriage, and precouple pregnancy is correlated with a relatively high divorce rate. No accurate statistics are available, but various studies and estimates suggest that the bride is pregnant in 50 to 75 per cent of all high school marriages, and that this pregnancy is the reason for the marriage.

Vocational Preparedness

Vocational preparedness is attained when a person is educated and trained sufficiently to undertake the support not only of him/herself but also of a family. Certainly, this kind of maturity is one of the most significant factors in marriage readiness, one of the most obvious and easily recognized, one of the simplest to use as a factor in deciding to marry—and one of the most commonly ignored. No state requires a statement of financial responsibility when marriage licenses are issued. Yet a leading cause of couple unhappiness and failure is economic difficulty.

The importance of economics to marriage cannot be overemphasized. If neither partner (but usually the husband in our society) has the training or education to provide satisfactorily for the family, no amount of personal compatibility or emotional maturity is likely to save them from couple problems.

Emotional Maturity
The emotionally mature person is relatively independent and self-directed. Self-direction and independence imply a good deal more than freedom from outside authority; a willingness to make decisions and to abide by their consequences is also involved. The emotionally mature person is other-centered rather than self-centered. S/he is able to accept adult responsibility for the well being of others as well as of him/herself. S/he is able to work toward group goals as well as individual ones. S/he is reality oriented rather than defense oriented. That is, s/he is able to acknowledge the reality of the present difficulties and to make realistic (or appropriate) efforts to resolve them. S/he is able to sacrifice short-term goals in order to achieve long-term goals. S/he is able to make heavy emotional investments in relations that are important to him/her, and yet, s/he is able to recover quickly from failure or disappointment. S/he can accept him/herself and others as s/he and they are in reality, rather than insisting on maintaining an idealized version of him/herself and those around him/her.

In short, in the emotionally mature person, the two-valued system (good/bad) of childhood is progressively replaced by a recognition and acceptance of the many valued complexities of real people living in a real world, where compromise is inevitable. The achievement of a full measure of emotional maturity is rare, of course. Emotional maturity, like all other aspects of the personality exists on a continuum—from the egocentric, black and white perception of the child to the other-centered, self-directed wisdom of the fully mature adult, with most adults falling somewhere on the two continuums between these two extremes.

Emotional support within marriage not only enhances the couple relation itself but also enhances accomplishment in other activities. Thus, the husband-wife relationship may become a source both of personal growth and material accomplishment. Conversely, failure to experience emotional support in marriage may spread to all other non-couple activities, with a resultant stunting of personality and increasing difficulties in all aspects of the person's social activities.

In short, emotional maturity involves a twofold process: and awareness of one's own needs and values, and an awareness of the needs and values of other people and of society at large. The emotionally mature person is able to fulfill his/her needs in ways that are appropriate to the situation. The more emotionally mature a person is, the greater the likelihood of a successful marriage.

Present Interests and Values
Studies have interestingly found that a shared interest in leisure activity has no correlation with couple happiness and that shared interests in community activity, money making, and material comfort have no correlation with couple happiness, but are actually correlated with a poor couple adjustment, as are shared interests in fame, success, travel, dancing, and drinking. The study found that a mutual LACK of interest in "a good time, commercial entertainment, and companionship to avoid loneliness" is highly correlated with success in marriage. The shared interests and values that did correlate with couple happiness, not surprisingly, were mutual interests, in sex, romantic love, children, and religion. The study also found that selfishness, cruelty, apathy, chronic illness, alcohol, and drug addiction, and a pre-marital expectation that marriage will change the other for the better, were all characteristics contributing to couple failure.

24

WHAT FACTORS COMPLICATE COUPLE SUCCESS?

"Money, Money can really ... Say there's 100% of people who got married. I would say that 40% got divorced because of money. Money is really a killer. Money could do that. It could put a lot of stress and pressure on you. You might have to sell your house." Brian.

Life would be so much simpler if we could arrange to fall in love and marry somebody suitable— with someone who wanted us as much as we wanted them, whom our friends and family approved of, who would not hurt us by ignoring or stepping on the love we offered.

Age Differences
Extremely powerful cultural norms specify who may love whom. One very explicit proscription is: Don't fall in love with someone who is old enough to be your father/mother or young enough to be your son/daughter. In other words: Love someone who is close to your own age.

Status Differences
A second complicating factor is the development of love is relative status. As more and more women enter the labor force it is not an unusual occurrence for a man and a woman of different status levels to fall in love. Love that emerges across status lines although it does occur with some frequency, is problematic from its inception.

Racial Differences
Regardless of how much parents love and trust their children of marriageable age, they cannot help but feel very concerned to hear, Guess who is coming to dinner? Love in the United States is generally depicted as blind, but not color blind. Whenever love develops between two people of different racial backgrounds, or different ethnic backgrounds, or religious or social classes, complications are bound to arise. Regardless of the rhetoric of tolerance, brotherhood, freedom, love, few observers of a cross-something (racial, social class, ethnic, religious) love relationship are able to remain objective. They are usually so persistent that are able to force the loving couple to consider potential complications to the relationship. Differences, particularly racial, are a complicating factor in love in this society and many others as well. Although racial tolerance does not represent

human beings at their best, it is a fact of social life to consider when one is becoming a lover. If one does not consider it, someone will remind him or her of it very quickly.

Different Experiences In The Expression Of Love

Love is something that involves the expression—verbal and nonverbal—of the feeling one has for the other person. In many families communication of any kind is not only problematic but also, practically speaking, nonexistent. On the other hand, in some families love and the expression of it is a way of life- families in which everyone is very demonstrable about his or her feelings.

Love can be complicated by the involvement of one person from a family that is trapped in an emotional poverty cycle in which love is just not expressed with a person from a family in which love is openly expressed. More likely than not the partner from the love deprived setting will want to learn how to express himself or herself. The partner from the love-satiated background should not expect miracles- it is hard to escape a cycle of emotional poverty. Even after the escape is seemingly complete, it is not unusual for temporary lapses, a reversion to the old non-expressive self.

CONCLUSIONS

If there were a successful rule of couple choice that emerges from this section, it would seem to be to look for a partner whose parents are happily married. And when we find such a person, to have a long and close relationship before marrying. Most of us acquire our basic mental image of what it means to be a husband and a father, or a wife or a mother, by watching the day-to-day and sometimes blow-by-blow interaction of our parents. Someone whose parents are happily married is likely to have been raised with functional role models; he or she has watched while couple difficulties were resolved successfully, and expects to be able to at least as well.

It is not enough to ask a prospective mate whether or not his parents or her parents are happily married: the question might be misinterpreted, and in any event, happiness is such a subjective category that the answer might be given in very different terms than we intended the question. Better to visit the family, as frequently as possible. To observe someone interacting with his mother, or with her father, is as instructive as watching how that person's father and mother interact.

It is less important to marry someone with whom you are in love than it is to marry someone with whom you feel comfortable, under a wide variety of situations. Someone who has a sense of who he or she is, and wants to be, and is comfortable with his/her self-image, will be more rewarding a partner than someone who is still trying to define himself/herself. Be sure that you can accept this person as s/he is, not hoping that s/he will grow out of some traits, or grow into others. It is certain that s/he will change (we all do), but not at all certain that a partner can direct that change.

Avoid marrying someone who seems to need you desperately. It is flattering to be needed, and some of us want to be needed, or believe that we do. It is easy to believe that such deep need is great love. But desperate need indicates that, sooner or later, you will be smothered by a relationship with a possessive and jealous partner.

For the rest, two people who share basic beliefs and values will have fewer conflicts than two people who have different values and beliefs. If religious beliefs are important to you, but not to the person you were thinking about marrying, explore how far apart your beliefs may be. If political activism is important to you, but not to the person you are marrying, explore that difference as well. Marriage is not a state of bliss, but a series of hard choices, and without some base of shared values and life goals, there will be little common ground on which to make those choices.

25   IS THERE A ONE AND ONLY?

Often when people have relationship difficulties and are unhappy, they feel they have picked the wrong person. They feel, "if only they would have picked "Mr. Right" then everything would have been okay. But this is a myth. The fact that there is no "one and only" in no way should cause persons not to screen carefully. Rather, it means that if one person doesn't measure up, assuming that your standards are realistic in terms of your own assets, there are many other persons who will. In other words, there's more than just one fish in the sea.

But when you're lonely and seem never to meet any eligible persons, it often seems discouraging and may lead to impulsive actions and bad decisions. But if you know what you are looking for, and your quest is realistic, and you make a systematic search, the results are likely to be favorable. In this world of over 4 billion people, there are undoubtedly many with whom you could fall in love and be happy. The trick is to know what you want and know what you can realistically expect and to then search until you find someone who not only fills the bill but also responds favorably to you in return.

26

"I LOVE YOU BUT I'M NOT IN LOVE WITH YOU"

There's a whole maneuver used by men and women to save face while wriggling out of relationships. It goes something like, "I love you but I'm not 'in love' with you. Now what kind of an image does that conjure up? And what does it really mean? Would it be more honest to say I have no sexual passionate feelings for you, just one's of affection, understanding and concern? And who of us would turn that down? And who of us would hate that idea? Who are we, each of us, and what does love mean to us?

> *Jennie and Bob were married for thirty years. They were now both in their early fifties, married when they were very young. They had two children, a boy and a girl who were successful professionals in their own right. While the children were growing up, the family led an active and involved life. They had a busy social life, had many friends, went on vacations together as a family, and developed their own careers. Now, though, Bob was feeling increasingly depressed. He didn't feel attracted to Jennie any longer. Their sex life had dwindled. He said he felt this way for a couple of years but thought it would go away. He went to therapy for about two years; hoping that his feelings would change or that he would get "fixed" but it didn't help that way. He felt that he loved Jennie but wasn't "in" love with her. He liked her as a person but didn't want to spend all that much time with her anymore. He felt that he was getting older, had spent a good portion of his life being a responsible, involved husband and father, and wanted to devote the rest of his life doing something else. There was no other woman in his life but he felt that maybe at some point there would be. He felt responsible for Jennie and said he would take care of her financially for the rest of her life though he didn't want to be a part of the rest of the her life.*

Perhaps the most common reason for the fading of romantic love is idealization of one's partner. In the excitement and joy of falling in love, most lovers idealize their partners and then later become disillusioned when limitations and faults become apparent. On the other hand, some lovers see their partners quite realistically and still love them passionately. Certainly couples in romantic relationships that endure for months or years are not likely to remain completely blind to each other's weaknesses.

Love may also fade because the love relationship itself does not live up to one or both partner's idealized version of it. If not all the elements of stereotypical "true love" are present, one person may drop out of the relationship and move on in his/her search for something closer to this fictional ideal.

Time itself may contribute to the fading of love. Time is necessary for lovers to get to know each other and to grow closer, but time can also reveal differences in goals, values, and interests that can create conflicts and cause the lovers to grow apart. Furthermore people change over time. Their needs desires at the beginning of a love relationship- the needs fulfilled by this particular loved one- can shift, so that they are no longer being met later in the relationship.

Although unrealistic views of love and change over time can be identified as "killers" of love, we really do not know all the reasons why love withers and dies. But die or fade it does, for a great many couples. The longer a couple is married, for example, the lower the score on Rubin's love scale suggesting how fragile and poorly understood romantic love really is.

But while romantic love usually loses its fight against time, companionate love does not. Instead of terminating a relationship when love fades, a couple could do worse than settle for a companionate love relationship. This is a choice that partners often make, in the sense that most marriages that endure are based on companionate rather than romantic love. After all, companionate love is usually more relaxing and harmonious than romantic love, and many older couples find it more appropriate. But companionate love may also have its risks. Retirement from passion may lead to a tranquil but dull relationship. And there is always the risk that one partner may meet someone new, fall in love, and abandon the comfortable love relationship in favor of the more exciting one. Certainly for most people who have experienced romantic love, settling for companionate love—however peaceful and tranquil it may be - is second best.

When we are in love, there are few situations that are more frustrating and painful than to hear our partner say, "I love you but I'm no longer in love with you." This statement represents perhaps the ultimate paradox in romantic love: the longing for permanence and ever-present danger of change.

This statement can mean one of two things. It may mean that the excitement, ecstasy, and sexual desires are no longer there. Romantic love has faded, but friendship and caring remain. A second possible meaning is opposite to the first: The sexual attraction and excitement endure, but respect and friendship have faded. In essence the person is still "in love" - at least in the sense of being sexually attracted- but not "in like."

Regardless of how the statement "I love you but I'm not in love with you" is interpreted, it is still likely to present a bewildering and painful problem for the person at the receiving end. For if the biochemical spark and excitement of romantic love have faded, it is usually impossible to rekindle them. And if the partner is no longer "in like," the possibility of maintaining anything but a temporary sexual relationship is remote. Either way, continuation of the relationship appears doomed.

Recently, couple therapists are reporting an increase in this type of situation — at least in middle-aged couples. This could possibly be explained by the longer life span in Western Civilization where couples conceivably can live with each other for fifty or more years. Or it could dictate individual psychological transitional crises. This, combined with an ideal of romantic love, could create disillusionment with a couple relationship that transforms into more of a friendship or even a brother-sister relationship over the years.

Often the couple will say, "Is this all there is?" So that this type of couple disillusionment may be a social, philosophical, and existential problem rather than an individual psychological one. Is it really realistic to expect couples to remain sexually and romantically interested in each other for possibly over fifty years?

27

CAN MEN AND WOMEN BE JUST FRIENDS OR DOES THE SEX THING GETS IN THE WAY? (THE HARRY AND SALLY QUESTION)

"Yes, you do! You're married and you have other men as your friends. But you cannot make sex with them!" Brian.

I've been a friend with Robert for the past ten years- just friends. We're both married to other people. We often talk about our marriages with each other— mainly complaining about our partners. His wife and my husband tolerate our friendship. At this point they feel okay about it although in the beginning they were a little suspicious. I never think of Robert in a sexual way, mainly, I guess, because I'm just not physically attracted to him.

We've been through a lot together: his father's death, my sister's divorce and I really value his opinion about a lot of issues. The other day he came over and he was looking at me in a funny way- in a way that he never did before. I asked him what was going on and he told me I looked really pretty. I had the distinct feeling that he was coming on to me and I feel so confused about it.

Michael and Joan met at a professional organization meeting. He was coming out of a four year committed relationship and she out of an eleven year marriage. From the beginning they became friends. Their relationship was always defined by them as platonic and while there were many moments of flirtation, basically, they were "just" good friends. They spoke every day on the phone and knew not only the intimate details of each other's lives but also how they each felt about most people and situations. They not only consoled each other through the ups and downs of the endings of their prior relationships but they also explored the nature of relationships and marriage for hours on the phone. He was afraid to make a commitment to a long-term relationship; she mistrusted her mate selection abilities. They spent many hours trying to figure out their dilemmas around these issues. Sometimes they would speak until the wee hours of the morning, laughing, crying, and learning about each other. They were best friends. They loved each other, cared for and about each other and enjoyed each other.

Most of their friends, feeling the positive energy between them, believed that they were involved in an affair and were just not "telling." But they were "just good friends." After a while they began to date others. They continued to discuss the men and women in their lives right down to the intimate sexual details. They knew everything about each other's feelings, thoughts, and lives.

One Saturday afternoon, they decided to spend the day together. They wanted to buy juicers for their new health kick and pillows for Michael's newly finished basement. They laughed and had fun playing in the stores, discussing their current age crisis and wondering about their health status. After dinner and a movie, they returned to Michael's home. Somehow they wound up watching TV in Michael's bed. This was not unusual. There were many times they had done this in the past, sharing a hotel room when they went to a conference, or watching TV in the same bed. While there were moments in the past when they were physically attracted to each other, neither one acted on these feelings. Joan tended to discount them, defining them as affectionate rather than sexual. Michael did the same.

Something was different this time though, and they moved toward each other in a new way. They made love for hours, touching, kissing, and feeling good with each other. The affection, love, caring, and feelings of comfortableness they had with each other in their friendship enhanced their lovemaking and both felt content and good sexually. But they were scared. The intensity of their affectionate feelings and their lovemaking brought up all sorts of scary feelings for both of them. Before they fell asleep, they promised each other that no matter what happened as a result of their lovemaking that they would remain friends. They hooked pinkies to seal their promise.

The next morning Joan had to leave early and she didn't have a chance to talk with Michael about what had happened until later that night. She felt weird all day. While she felt so good about their lovemaking, she also felt numb and scared of what it all meant. He felt like he didn't quite know what had happened.

The next night Michael decided that his scared feelings meant that he was not ready to make a commitment to Joan and he told her that they should go back to being "just good friends." He told her that he still wanted to date other women and that he didn't want to hurt her in the process because he knew she would not be in a sexual relationship that was not monogamous. Joan didn't understand why he was doing this; it seemed like they were really good together; they really cared about each other and enjoyed each other sexually. She thought they should just let the newly defined relationship develop and see where it took them. She was scared also. She had not dated very much; she initially was not attracted to Michael and wondered if the attraction she felt now would be sustained over the long run. She had doubts around whether he would be faithful to her long term. She had doubts about whether she could be in a long-term relationship herself.

But she felt that they had a lot together— friendship, love, caring, fun, and now, sexual intimacy; they agreed on life goals and life values; they shared professions; they shared views about their children. It seemed weird to her that he was saying what he was saying.

She thought that by backing away from this new intimacy in their relationship, he was reinforcing his fears of intimacy and commitment. She once again began to question her mate selection capabilities and her capacities to choose someone who could be in a long-term relationship and how this fit into her own abilities around intimacy.

A complete discussion of love must consider the possibility of love relationships that are free from sexual desire. A platonic relationship between a male and a female involves neither romance nor sex. Studies show that the majority of college students believe platonic relationships can exist, but when they are asked to describe the nature of the relationship, their illustrations almost always fall into specific categories such as the following:

Opposite Sex Friends Tend To Be:

Dating Rejects. The individual was dated at one time but is no longer viewed as datable for various reasons.

Pseudo-Family. The individual has grown up with the person in a close, "brother-sister" type relationship.

The Committed. The friend is going steady, is engaged or married, and is therefore not a dating possibility.

The Different. The person is of a different race, religion, age, etc.

These categories are essentially safe relationships in which the platonic friend is not perceived in the role of a possible love interest. It is always possible that the safe factor may be destroyed if the individual starts to define the friend in a romantic light. But essentially, the friend is usually defined as platonic because it is believed that he can't be a romantic figure. Furthermore, with few restrictions, close-paired relationships are restricted to the unmarried person. Once a person is married, friendships are either between members of the same sex or between married couples. In American society, a close friendship between a married man and a married woman is viewed with suspicion. What the couple may view as a platonic friendship will often be viewed as romantic or sexual by others. The implication of this belief is obvious. What it means is that by the early adult years, persons must, in most cases, exclude members of the opposite sex from close personal paired friendship.

However, upon exploring this question further, it becomes much more complicated. In modern day society, with more and more women entering the work force, men and women often work shoulder to shoulder in many different situations. Although many people don't like to mix business with pleasure, the reality of the situation is that often men and women become friends at the work place. Many deals are made over lunch; many projects started over a drink. Some may be married; some may even be physically attracted to each other. Some wind up having affairs—usually short-lived ones for people are generally very reluctant to leave their partners under these situations, although some will. In several cases, though, the friends have acknowledged their physical attraction to each other, have acknowledged their commitment to their partners, and have decided to keep their friendship exactly that—a friendship.

Jim and Jenny met each other at a professional organization meeting. Both were interested in many of the same activities. They went for coffee and began sharing experiences. It seemed like they had so much in common and could have talked for hours. Jenny was married and Jim was divorced, but seeing someone. They called each other after the conference and decided to work together on a few projects that both were interested in. After some time they decided to attend a training seminar together.

The seminar lasted for three days during which time they were constantly together—talking and sharing ideas and experiences. Jenny felt like Jim was one of her girlfriends—with one exception, she was physically attracted to him. Jim felt like he could tell Jenny anything— even about sexual affairs with other women. He felt so comfortable with her—with one exception, he was physically attracted to her. After dinner one night, they decided to go out dancing—to get some physical exercise after sitting through the seminar all day. While dancing, she felt him pull her closer and was very much aware of his lips in her hair. He felt her soft body against his own and wanted to pull her even closer. They knew they were in trouble. They said they needed to talk and sat down at the table. Both acknowledged how easy it would be to "be" with each other and how attracted they were to each other. But they decided to remain friends. And so they did. Now four years later, they're still friends—closer than ever and they feel comfortable and sure about their earlier decision. Now they can flirt with each other and play with other and care about and for each other, knowing that they are perfectly safe with each other.

28

NOW THAT I'VE FOUND
A POTENTIAL MATE,
WHAT PART DOES DATING PLAY?

"A boy and a girl or a girl and a girl or a boy and a boy go out to a romantic place. They go someplace. The boy or the girl takes the person or persons, people out to lunch or a movie. But, you don't want to take them to a Chinese restaurant. You should take them to a movie, I would say someplace romantic. Not too romantic. A Movie, a swimming pool, no, not a swimming pool. I would say a movie. Oh! Down by a lake, not up in an airplane. That's not romantic. By a lake or in a movie." Brian.

"Dating" in the United States, while relatively informal, guides mate selection in an orderly way, with a sequence that usually begins with casual dating and then moves to serious dating, engagement, and marriage. Although a wide variety of alternatives prevail, most marriages in our society follow this pattern.

In recent years, traditional dating patterns in our society have gone by the wayside. Dating has undergone marked changes designed to counteract its sexist, hypocritical, an anxiety producing nature. In short, the more informal practices of getting together and casual dating have replaced the more formal pattern of traditional dating for many young people. Getting together may involve joining informally with a group to listen to music, play volleyball, roller-skate, have a party, or whatever. Such groups tend to develop spontaneously, and the male is no longer responsible for planning the dating activity or picking up the tab. The emphasis is on meeting people in an informal setting and getting to know them as persons. If a specific couple finds that they are attracted to each other, they may pair off.

Relationships progress from casual dating to serious dating. Casual dating typically involves informally arranged meetings, such as getting together during a coffee break or for lunch. Such dates do not involve the commitment of more than a small amount of time, and neither party feels rejected if the other loses interest. In more formal dating patterns, the male or female may feel hurt and rejected of s/he cannot arrange for a second date. Casual dating basically serves as a screening device for people who are attracted to each other but wish to get better acquainted before deciding whether to continue or terminate the encounter.

The transition from casual to serious dating is accompanied by a number of important changes. The relationship during serious dating is characterized by increasing reports of caring and/or love feelings, the sense of belonging with the partner, and public recognition of the pair as constituting a definite unit. Moreover, the transition to serious dating is usually marked by an increase in conflict and negativity between partners. In this stage, couples also recognize the seriousness or depth of their feelings toward each other, can be sexually intimate, discuss the possibility of marriage, and begin to plan their future together. The attraction to the partner now derives from need satisfactions as well as from the attractions of the previous stage.

During serious dating, the partners become increasingly interdependent and emerging exclusivity - with respect to what activities, including sex, will be shared with the partner only- tends to become a source of conflict. During this stage, jealousy can sharply increase and tends to be resolved as conflicts concerning exclusivity become resolved. Conflicts can also arise over differences in goals, values, and personality characteristics. This is also a period when each partner tends to make attributions about the self, such as I'm in love, I care about things that happen to my partner. Our relationship is special. I would like to spend the rest of my life with him/her. We can face the world together.

There are several types of dating arrangements. For example, one couple might follow the typical progression from encounter to casual dating to serious dating. Another might go directly to serious dating after the first encounter. Some moved from one step to another without serious conflict, while others reached transitional decision-making points where considerable conflict occurred before they proceeded with the relationship. It could be that conflict is a common accompaniment to feelings of love in close relationships, especially as the partners become increasingly knowledgeable about each other and as incompatibilities surface. Such conflicts or lovers quarrels function either to force a compromise and resolution of the conflict or termination of the relationship. Thus, lover's quarrels need not be destructive but may actually help the couple work out misunderstandings, disagreements, and differences. However, open and serious conflicts during the stage of serious dating do not serve the relationship well.

Assuming that a relationship survives and leads to increasing interdependence, closeness, and commitment during the serious dating stage, the next step usually involves engagement, cohabitation, or perhaps both.

29 SHOULD WE GET ENGAGED?

Traditionally, engagement represented the final stage in a couple's movement toward marriage. Essentially, it is a ritual symbolizing exclusive commitment to one's partner in terms of a public announcement of one's intent to marry. Interestingly enough, the transition from serious dating to engagement is less pronounced than that from casual to serious dating.

The institution of engagement in our society serves chiefly to help the couple determine whether or not they should marry. As such, it is an invaluable contributor to eventual couple success. During the engagement period, each person has a chance to explore the other's unique qualities and to consider whether those qualities are compatible with his/her own. In addition, the engaged couple learns new meanings of loyalty to each other and new kinds of social interactions with relatives, friends, acquaintances, and future in-laws. Finally, the couple are given time to recognize that they have significant differences (if they have) and to break the engagement. Skipping the engagement and marrying immediately is highly inadvisable and very risky in terms of the success of the marriage and the happiness of the individuals.

As a final step before marriage, engagement serves a number of functions that may overlap with but are somewhat different from those in the serious dating stage.

Engagement Provides:

- Provides a time to agree upon and work out fundamental living arrangements. Where and how will the couple live? Will both work? How do they plan to spend their income?
- Provide a time to reexamine and agree upon both short-term and long-term goals and the methods they plan to use for achieving these goals.
- Provides a time to get better acquainted with each other's families and to agree upon how they will relate to in-laws and to each other's friends.

- Provides a time to make a final check—of each other in terms of common interests, values, goals, comfort in each other's company, and compatibility in general.
- Provides a time for working out final details of the wedding plans. Will they have a church wedding? Will the wedding for formal or informal? Who will be invited? Who will give the bride away? Who will be the best man, maid of honor? What about rehearsals? What sort of honeymoon, if any, will they have?

While the engagement period is often thought of as a happy one in which each partner looks forward to the coming marriage, researchers have found that the feelings reported to occur during engagement span the range from love, belonging, extreme happiness, and excitement to ambivalence, conflict, negativity, and anxiety. This suggests that this stage of the relationship may be rather turbulent and traumatic. Not only do the partners experience conflict in themselves and between each other, but also they may encounter conflict with each other's families, who may disapprove of the marriage. Researcher Kando has pointed out that engagement is an expression of love, commitment, and joyful anticipation of the marriage. It may be very meaningful not only to the engaged couple, but also to their parents, friends, and relatives, who are brought into contact with each other.

If the engagement period is to be most effective, it should be comparatively long- from six months to two years. A classic study by Burgess and Cottrell found that more than half of the couples that had been engaged for less than three months before their marriage rated their subsequent couple adjustment as "poor." Among those who had been engaged for two years or more, only one in ten rated their couple adjustment as "poor." A year's engagement yielded an 80 percent chance of either "good" or "fair" couple adjustment. Another classic study and the most extensive to date also relates engagement success to marriage success, and assumes that the adjustments made during the engagement are productive of the kind of adjustments that will be made during marriage.

30   WHAT ABOUT LIVING TOGETHER?

"No! You should not live with the person. I think you should not get a baby before you are married. Let's just say this. Let's say I just make sex with someone, and the lady gets a baby. I would just say. I don't want a baby. I do not want it. You don't want to get stuck with a baby and you don't want to put it in an orphanage because you don't want to." Brian.

"I just don't get that feeling. I really think you shouldn't live with a person before you're married. I just don't think so. You should go over their house for dinner a couple of times— 3, 4, 5 times. Definitely over 2. Over 2. I don't think you should live with them." Brian.

Today, more and more young people believe that a trial marriage by way of cohabitation provides a far better test and anticipatory socialization for marriage than a ritualistic exchange of rings. However, there is another side to the issue of engagement versus cohabitation. Research findings fail to support the notion that cohabitation provides a better test and better preparation for marriage than engagement. Furthermore, there is no evidence that couples that cohabit prior to marriage have happier marriages than those who have presumably followed the more conventional sequence from dating through engagement to marriage.

Are Participants In Cohabitating Relationships More Likely To Marry Each Other Than Are Persons Who Are Going Together?

The percentage of cohabitants who eventually marry each other is not known. However, researcher Risman found that there were no differences in rates of marriage or breakup between couples living together and those going together. If we assume that the findings from this study are typical, then the answer to this question is no.

Are Students Who Cohabit Likely To Marry Sooner Than Couples Going Together?

Cohabitation appeared to speed up the rate of relationship development. For example, he found that cohabitating couples exhibited greater intimacy than the couples going together, even though none of the couples in either group knew each other longer. Among those who eventually married, those who had cohabitated married sooner than those who had not. So the answer to the second question is yes.

Do Couples Who Have Cohabitated Prior To Marriage Have Happier Marriages Than Those Who Have Not?

Research has shown that there are no differences in couple satisfaction between those who had cohabitated and those who had not. Also there were no differences in divorce rates. Cohabitators differed in the types of problems that led to conflict in their marriages. For example, cohabitators tended to bicker less but reported more conflicts over adultery, alcohol, drugs, and autonomy than those who had not cohabitated.

However, recent research found that divorced persons who had cohabitated with a new partner after the divorce judged their remarriages to be more successful than did couples who had not cohabitated. In the actual assessment of their marriages, the cohabitators scored higher than the cohabitators on such measures of family strength as positive communication, closeness, promoting each other's welfare, and happiness. So, perhaps cohabitation serves a somewhat different function for those who have been married before than it does for the never-marrieds. However, more research is needed to replicate this finding.

To summarize this section, the answer to the original question of whether cohabitation makes for a happier marriage appears to be no.

Although engagement today does tend to be more informal than in the past, possibly because many of the functions formerly reserved for the engagement period are now carried out during the stage of serious dating, it does involve a sense of mutual commitment that is lacking in cohabitation.

When one of the cohabitators tires of the arrangement, s/he simply moves on. If we were to criticize traditional engagement, it might be on the grounds of too much commitment and too little experience to ensure the couple is really compatible and ready for marriage. On the other hand, if we were to criticize cohabitation, it could well be on the ground that it leads to too much experience of a rather superficial type and too little commitment.

31

WHAT IS PREMARITAL COUNSELING LIKE?

Traditional counseling of engaged couples has focused on sexual adjustment, relations with in-laws, wedding plans, and special problems such as pregnancy. In recent years, this approach has been implemented and enriched by:

- **Helping each partner better understand himself/herself and the other person.**
- **Helping the couple better understand the nature and quality of their present relationship.**
- **Pinpointing some of the problems they are likely to encounter if they marry.**
- **Assessing their readiness for marriage at this time.**
- **Improving needed communications, conflict resolving, and decision-making skills.**

Pre-marital counseling consists of a series of interviews (typically two to five), but sometimes more that you and your partner have with a counselor. Usually the opportunity is available for both joint and individual interviews with the counselor. Although the counselor may suggest topics to consider, you and your partner decide how extensively you wish to explore each topic. In these interviews, you can also ask questions and discuss other matters that concern either or both of you. This exploration can be very valuable for partners who plan to live together, whether in formal marriage or without a wedding ceremony. Some counselors provide for couples to return for follow up interviews during the first months of marriage. Sometimes, counseling is provided to a group of couples that are all planning to marry at about the same time.

A good pre-marital counseling procedure is more concerned with the interaction between you and your partner than with a rigid schedule or set of answers. A counselor may encourage you to think about your decision in new ways, but it is ultimately your decision about how you will arrange your marriage or living together. This section addresses pre-marital counseling; however, it could also be applied to any couple who is thinking of making a long-term commitment to each other.

Pre-marital counseling is available from many professional counselors. Religious organizations, pastoral counseling centers, and teachers of marriage and the family courses can assist you in locating qualified professionals who provide pre-marital counseling. The American Association of Marriage and Family Therapists (AAMFT) in Washington, D.C. can also refer you to qualified couple counselors in your locality.

Expenses of pre-marital counseling vary widely. Some religious groups provide pre-marital counseling at no charge, as part of the ministry to the membership and the community, while others may suggest that you make a contribution you consider appropriate. Other counselors have a set schedule of fees for each counseling interview. It is always appropriate to discuss the matter of fees and other expenses when inquiring about pre-marital counseling.

Whether you intend to have a very informal, simple service or an elaborate wedding, pre-marital counseling is very important. If you plan to have your wedding solemnized by a minister, priest, or rabbi who also provides pre-marital counseling, then some additional interview time will be needed to consider the meanings of the wedding ceremony in that tradition and to plan details of the ceremony. Some religious counselors will be cooperative if you want to modify a standard wedding service or include parts that you have special significance for you and your partner.

Some counselors with special training use psychological tests and inventories as part of the counseling process prior to marriage or living together. Some counselors may share test and inventory data with the couple in counseling and use it as a basis for some of the interview discussions.

No test is able to determine whether you should or should not marry, nor can a test predict that you will or will not be successful in living with a particular person. You should not rely on any purported test for couple success, which is published in a general newspaper or magazine, nor should you depend upon tests to replace your personal ability to decide and plan for your lives together. Tests can be useful in pre-marital counseling, but they can easily be given a degree of precision or infallibility that they do not deserve. Some pre-marital counseling procedures will include psychological testing but other equally good procedures may not include testing at all.

Unfortunately, the only pre-marital preparation most states require for marriage is proof of age and a blood test. The blood test is minimal since it usually checks only for the presence of syphilis prior to granting a marriage license. It is very desirable however, for both the man and the woman to have a physical examination by a physician prior to the wedding. In most cases, it will simply conform the good health of each person, but occasionally, an examination may detect a physical condition that should be treated. This is also an opportunity to plan contraceptive procedures and to secure information about genetic factors if such has not been done earlier.

Good pre-marital preparation cannot guarantee that your marriage will succeed. Only you and your mate can provide this guarantee. However, it can assist you and your partner to avoid potential difficulties and to develop ways to find greater joy together in your marriage.

The long-term effects of pre-marital counseling have not been determined, although many young people say they do find it helpful. Interestingly, it appears that cohabitating couples gain more from the counseling than engaged ones do. Perhaps non-cohabitators are not yet quite as ready to face the realities that lie ahead. Whatever the case, the purpose of pre-marital counseling is not to talk the couple out of getting married.

A relatively new approach to marriage preparation is engaged encounter programs, usually consisting of weekend sessions sponsored by churches or service agencies in the community. Such programs are designed to help couples become more thoroughly prepared for marriage.

Medical Examination

Final preparation for marriage should include pre-marital medical counseling that extends beyond the cursory examinations required by most states. A complete physical examination may disclose problems that the person should be aware of before making a final commitment to the marriage. The medical examination may determine if one of the couple is unable to have children. The couple should also have information on sexuality and birth control.

EXERCISE: Assessment

- How closely related are your long-term interests?
- How closely related are your life goals?
- How closely related are your moral standards?
- Do you respect each other's ideals, or feel they are trivial?
- Do you agree on vocational choice?
- Do you agree on residence?
- Do you accept each other as they really are, or do you anticipate important change?
- Do each of you feel proud of each other, or does one feel constrained to excuse or explain the other's appearance or conduct?
- If each of you were to list the things s/he most likes to do, or would be most reluctant to give up, how many activities would occur on both lists?
- Do you like each other's close friends, or are they bored with them?
- Do you like each other's close relatives?
- How do each of you feel after they have been together—elated or depressed? relaxed, and confident, or moody and uneasy?
- Can you be together with no sense of strain?
- After a date do you find yourself reminiscing with pleasure or brooding over what might have been said to make a point?
- Is your satisfaction with each other broad enough to sustain through marriage?
- Do each of you have some awareness of the mundane necessities of allocating income among the necessary expenditures—an evaluation of what is available to spend and what each wants to spend it on—should certainly also be included in your assessment of their compatibility.
- Attitude toward religion is also important in assessing compatibility, since religion often plays a very significant role in couple interaction.

32   NOW THAT YOU'RE MARRIED

Keep your eyes wide open before marriage, half shut afterwards (Benjamin Franklin).

Now marriage is, after all, just a way of living— i.e. a type of life style. We know enough at least on a rational level that we don't expect life to be all sunshine and roses. But somehow on an emotional level we do expect marriage to be that way. People who are accustomed to bickering with everyone are shocked when they find that they bicker with their wives. Women who have found everything somewhat disappointing are surprised and pained when marriage proves itself no exception. Most of the complaints about the institution of holy matrimony arise not because it is worse than the rest of life, but because it is not incomparably better.

Before marriage, people in love have a tendency to emphasize the similarities in their ways of thinking rather than the differences. It is easy for a couple to idealize each other and to impute attitudes that may not exist. After they are launched upon life as a married couple, differences in personality traits and value systems will tend to become more apparent. Gradually the two may recognize that they are not in such close agreement on everything as they had thought during the engagement.

There are reasons for this almost universal feeling of disillusionment about marriage. One is that we are taught to expect too much from it. But even if we have become extremely cynical about marriage in general, we are apt to be disillusioned about our own, because most of us marry while we are in the throes of love and passion. The sexual excitement, the uncertainties and novelties of the new relationship, actually lift us out of ourselves for a time. With the best will in the world we cannot during the falling in love stage show ourselves to our beloved as we really are, can't allow them to see us in our everyday personality. We are quite not genuinely our everyday selves at this period. We are more intense, more vital than usual. Moreover we see ourselves through the eyes of our beloved. Unconsciously we match our feeling about ourselves with the glorified impression s/he has formed of us.

This excited state of mind cannot endure the protracted association of marriage. The thrilling sexual tension that normally keeps engaged couples in a state of fervid and delighted expectation abates with frequent, satisfying intercourse. The element of uncertainty is dissipated, and there is no doubt that a goal we have not yet won is more intriguing than one which is wholly ours. Sooner or later when flamboyant anticipations of commitment and betrothal give way to the sober realities of marriage, we lapse back into our ordinary selves. Fortunately we can surpass ourselves during emotional crises without seriously depleting our reserves. We can run from a tiger very fast indeed but if we made that speed habitual, we would soon collapse entirely. Walking is the most practical speed for most activities, and marriage too must be paced at the rate of our usual temperament. This inevitable change of pace, slowing down, is what we call disillusionment and it happens in most, if not all, marriages. Our disillusionment does not proceed wholly or perhaps even primarily from the unromantic facts we learn about our partner in the course of daily observation. It comes largely from our bored recognition of the same old self within our own breast. Our newfound charm and prowess and glamour evaporate when we can no longer read them in a worshipping gaze, when we are no longer stimulated by the desire for conquest.

The beginning portions of this book have shown that the routes whereby couples approach marriage are multiple and varied. We have tried to point out the issues associated with mate selection and love. It seems likely that some persons exercise rationality in their selection of partners and approach marriage with realistic expectations. At the other extreme are couples caught up in an overwhelming attraction for one another. Some of these relationships develop essentially without exploitation and involve intense idealization of each partner by the other. In others, one partner is clearly dominant, with the disadvantaged partner more or less successfully concealing the already present pain the relationship produces. Some couples are trapped into marriage by pregnancy. Some appear to result primarily from the pressures exerted by partners and friends, and the lack of a better alternative. Some defy explanation.

For most couples, though, marriage represents a sharp break with conditions of prior living. The marriage ceremony endorses whatever relationship already exists and, often, propels them into a twenty-four hour a day physical and emotional intimacy for which they are not wholly prepared. Marriages seldom are scheduled to coincide with readiness for full intimacy but are arranged, instead, in terms of less relevant criteria such as graduation from college, attaining the minimum legal age, passing the bar and so on. We know a famous professor who made his decision to marry on whether or not he passed his comprehensive examinations! It should not be surprising, then, that the sudden transition occasioned by the wedding ceremony is accompanied by both bliss and strain from most young couples.

Researcher Waller describes the early weeks of marriage as infused with erotically tinged euphoria. To the degree idealization has developed during courtship, each partner carries into marriage a romanticized conception of what the other is like. Each has been living somewhat beyond himself, on cloud nine as it were. It seems wonderful to be marrying such an extraordinary person as the partner appears to be and, if the partner is so exceptional, then one must also be special to merit such a partner.

Many forces operate in the pre-marital period to enhance the egos and general well being of the couple. To have found a partner at all represents success in the competition for mates. To have found such an ideal partner produces something akin to a mild, continuing intoxication. Then as the sexual relationship progresses, there is the overwhelming desire for complete fulfillment. As with other forms of fulfillment, the anticipation, the fantasy and the accompanying feelings probably are as important the achievement itself. Finally, the approval and vicarious participation of family and friends in the relationship brings additional psychic rewards. One's position has shifted a little closer to the center of the universe, and one experiences emotions that surely are reserved for only the very special.

This euphoria continues into the early weeks of marriages. Moreover it is reinforced by the excitement of the newly married status, the acquiring of new possessions, the moving into new quarters, and the establishing of new routines. According to Waller this anesthetizes each partner against the too early and too violent intrusion of preexisting habit patterns of the non-meshing habits of the partner. Thus, a man, fussy about food can eat undercooked eggs without the gastrointestinal spasms that would otherwise be produced. Similarly, the young wife who finds that her husband wears his underwear for three days and then throws them under the bed is not immediately overcome with revulsion. Locked in one another's arms, in their fantasies, in their new status, and in the interest and approval of others, most couples experience- whether or not they take a wedding trip - an initial blissful adjustment, which merits the sentimental term **HONEYMOON.**

Stage 1 The Happy Honeymoon Phase

"Yes, this is my sister, Barbara and my brother-in-law, Steve. They got married. I was the ring bearer. After they got married, they went to the Bahamas or Jamaica. I'm not sure. But that's a honeymoon. After you're married you go someplace. You're there and you're happy that you got married. Maybe you make sex, I don't know." Brian.

In the continuing romantic glow and excitement that accompanies the wedding and honeymoon, the couple are likely to experience optimism about any future problems and to expect the dramatic and tingling qualities of the relationship to continue evermore. The couple tend too tell themselves that despite minor irritations and problems that may arise on the honeymoon, their own relationship is uniquely blessed. Regardless of the past experiences of others, they expect their romantic high to continue indefinitely. It is this romantic bliss coupled with a time out from life that helps the couple through the early days of marriage. Thus stage I is often referred to as the "Happy Honeymoon" period.

Although a marriage cannot endure on fun alone, the happy honeymoon phase appears to be an important one in helping to establish a stable foundation for marriage. The couple's knowledge that they can enjoy their time alone together helps them to weather the difficult times ahead and maintain their relationship as a source of satisfaction to them both.

Even during this period, however, the couple moves toward a modus vivendi. Our social system does not provide rigidly structured roles into which husband and wife must fit, but depends upon the attraction between them to see them through the development of roles appropriate to their situation and which will enhance their social and economic status. In other words, there are large areas of couple behavior, which must be defined in a short time.

Paradoxically, the so-called honeymoon period also is characterized by the unusual sensitivity of each partner to the behavior of the other. The euphoria alternates with periods of excessive sensitivities, hurt and shock at actual or alleged slights. If idealization frequently accompanies courtship, so does doubt— of self, of partner, and of the relationship. To the degree to which love serves as a rationalization of the movement toward marriage, the partner who has these feelings may react violently to their confirmation in the marriage. The first time, for example, that the husband comes home too tired to go out with his wife may constitute irrefutable proof that he does not love her. The first time that the wife crawls into bed and goes promptly to sleep may signal to the husband that he should have heeded his doubts about getting married in the first place.

Stage 2 Disillusionment and Regrets

Question To Brian: So, what if you're married, and your wife wants to kiss you more than you want to kiss her, what do you do?
"It's __my__ lips! So, I would just move back or leave. And especially if I told her fifty million times and she didn't listen."

Question: And what if you wanted to kiss her more than she wanted to kiss you, what would you do?
"She would just say back off. And I would. My 'harmones' are not ready yet." Brian.

Stage 2, Disillusionment and Regrets, is referred to as the honeymoon-is-over syndrome. It is characterized by conflicts, regrets, and ambivalence about the marriage. Now one or both partners feel that they have made a terrible mistake. They feel trapped in a marriage from which escape is difficult, if not impossible. Even though sexual and other aspects of the marriage may be satisfying, the hopes and fantasies of the courtship and honeymoon periods are replaced with feelings of disillusionment and disappointment. Yet, for the marriage to survive, the couple must surmount this second stage. The fact that many couples do not make it past this hurdle is attested to by the high incidence of divorce during the first year of marriage.

Stage 2 can perhaps be better understood in light of the circumstances of romantic love. Some degree of disappointment seems inevitable as the sense of perfect oneness begins to fade and the idealized and unrealistic view of the partner and the relationship give way to more objective perceptions. Unfortunately the intimacy of marriage tends to exaggerate differences that were formerly obscured and the partner's real or alleged faults tend to be blown out of proportion. Long cherished illusions are now shattered and fantasies go unfulfilled. Now the previously inseparable lovebirds get on each other's nerves and seem to be continually disagreeing about something. The tendency is to blame each other for not living up to what was promised or even for not behaving the way the person behaved during courtship. Often the partners experience a mounting sense of frustration and anger at being trapped in such a stupid situation— in a marriage that obviously isn't working. And the combination of emotional turmoil and fighting leads them to say, and sometimes do, things that make the continuation of the relationship even more difficult.

One study found that whereas in stage 1 the couple has the pleasurable task of discovering their similarities, in stage 2 they must come to grips with their differences. Stage 2 also involves mutual disapproval, which seems even more painful because it is unexpected. When people are falling in love, they usually get a concentrated dose of approval, often expressed in such statements as, "I really enjoy being around you because you make me feel so good about myself." Now the appreciation turns to criticism and the characteristic complaint becomes, "You make me feel so bad." It is during this phase that the couple learns to appreciate both their positive and negative impact on each other, especially their vulnerability to hurt.

Unfortunately some couples never recover from the hurt or from the shock of discovering that their marriage will never be what they assumed, expected, or hoped it would be. When the feeling of having been deceived and betrayed by one's partner is added to the picture, there may be little likelihood of the relationship surviving. The disillusionment and hurt may simply be too great to overcome.

Happily, most couples do succeed in outgrowing stage 2. They work through their disillusionment and disappointment, their resentment at being trapped, their differences in goals and values, and their temptations to blame and hurt each other. Then they are free to accept each other as persons and to perceive and appreciate each other's good qualities.

Stage 3 Accommodation

Stage 3, Accommodation, involves adjusting one's expectations for the relationship to realistic levels and rekindling the biochemical spark that originally brought them together. It means building a realistic and durable foundation based on the romantic love and positive qualities of the early days of the relationship.

Of course, this is much easier said than done, for the task requires mastery of the basic ingredients of intimate relationships described in the prior chapter, including effective communication, mutual self-disclosure, and skillful conflict resolution.

By this time it is probably apparent that the transition from singlehood to marriage is by no means easy for most people. And we have not even mentioned the personal problems of adjusting to a changed identity, to new roles and responsibilities, to less freedom in relating to members of the opposite sex, and to the many other demands that accompany the couple union. In short, being married is different—very different.

The opportunities for rebuffs and slights in early marriage are many. Moreover, marriage forces upon people an intimacy, which is not all erotic. Husbands cannot escape confrontation with the paraphernalia attending menstruation or with hair curlers and the washing of lingerie. Many wives must handle dirty socks and underwear and clean up the bathroom, which has been turned into a swamp during their husband's showers. Both sexes must content with messy toothpaste tubes and catsup bottles—rendered that way by "inconsiderate" partners.

Waller defined the honeymoon as that period in the psychic adjustment of the couple while illusion lasts. Eventually, she thought, the opposition between idealization on the one hand and the intrusion of humdrum reality on the other yields to reality. Inherent in this transition is some disillusionment, both with the partner and with oneself. If the partner is not so different from others, then the special desirability that was imputed to oneself must be illusory also. The shattering of dreams is painful and the onset of disillusionment sets the stage for conflict. When disillusionment occurs, conflict develops. No one enjoys being hurt and the marriage partner is not only the most available target but is also by a perverse sort of logic responsible for one's plight. What is more natural than to attack?

33   THE COUPLE CONTRACTS

The Couple Contract

There are basically three levels for understanding marriages. The Marriage Contract is where each partner has his or her vague awareness of terms that s/he believes his or her partner has agreed to. Generally speaking, the two mates' contracts are usually quite different. Each contract consists of conscious and unconscious expectations of the relationship, of what the individual wants from his or her partner and what he or she will give in return. Some of the terms may be at odds with others, thus producing inconsistency so that contradictory messages are given to the partner. When one partner perceives that the other partner is not fulfilling the terms of the contract, usually the partner then tries to correct the breach of the contract by reacting in characteristic ways such as becoming angry, withdrawing etc. Here it is helpful for the couple to try to first specify what their couple contract is and then make attempts to move toward having a single contract whose terms are known to both of you. There probably will not be agreement on every term. Where there are differences, they should be responded to and respected and compromises are to be worked out.

Upon first glance at a couple's interaction, the relationship appears random, one person simply responding to the other. However, if one examines the couple over a period of time, dominant patterns can be discerned. It is also important to note that profiles for any individual may vary markedly with different mates or at different times in the couple life cycle.

The marriage contract concept, along with the interactional contract and behavioral contract, is helpful in aiding a couple to understand their dynamics. In addition, it suggests points and approaches for increasing information to the couple about their relationship. In this way, the couple will understand their relationship on a conscious, aware level.

The Interactional Contract

In the interactional contract or script, the two partners collaborate to establish and maintain a method of achieving sufficient gratification of their biological and psychological needs as well as their adult and remaining infantile wishes. The marriage must accomplish this without arousing too much defensive anxiety or aggression that the marriage as a unit capable of fulfilling its goals and purposes is destroyed. The interactional contract deals with how a couple together tries to fulfill each partner's separate goals and purposes. It is the how and not the what. The interactional contract provides the operational field in which each struggles with the other to achieve fulfillment of his or her own individual contract. It is the place where each partner tries to achieve his or her own objectives and force the other to behave in accordance with his or her own design of the marriage.

If the interactional contract is unclear, the couple should work on making the interactional contract and the couples' behavior more conscious. The increased awareness on the part of both partners automatically works toward their arriving at a new single contract that provides for healthier interactions.

The Behavioral Contract
The behavioral profile refers to the prevalent way in which one mate relates to the other. The behavioral contract is the contract working at the most obvious level. It is the working through of the day-to-day behaviors that will maintain the routines of relationships demand. For example, it is the overt manifestation of who mows the lawn, who washes the dishes, who cooks. Basically the couple contracts make understandable what the couple conflict is about on superficial as well as intrapsychic and couple-system levels. When couples argue about typical complaints such as money, sex, time, past injuries, child rearing, former partners, or friends, the use of the contract concept makes it possible to go beyond these complaints to more basic issues which may include power, inclusion-exclusion, closeness-distance, and passive-assertive diameters, absence of love, caring etc. Thus, the couple is in a better position to determine whether to deal with the symptom or with the common underlying etiological factor that may cause several symptoms to surface.

EXERCISE: The Couple Contract

This exercise is to help you examine your conscious and unconscious couple contract. It is separated into three sections. In order to refresh your memory about couple contracts, read P. 168.

The first section is the Couple Contract. In this section, please try to define what you see your couple contract to be. When you married, what did you agree to? What are your expectations? Of yourself? Of your partner? What do want from your partner? Please be as specific as you can.

_____

_____

_____

_____

_____

_____

_____

_____

_____

_____

_____

_____

_____

_____

After you have finished specifying your own Couple Contract, specify what you think is your mate's couple contract—what s/he thinks s/he has agreed to, what s/he expects from himself/herself, what s/he expects of you. Again, please be as specific as you can.

_____

_____

_____

_____

_____

_____

_____

_____

_____

_____

_____

_____

_____

_____

_____

_____

_____

_____

_____

Now ask your partner to fill out the same form and then compare contracts. You will notice that you probably have some items that are similar and some that are different. Try to move toward developing one contract where each of you knows the terms.

_____

_____

_____

_____

_____

_____

_____

_____

_____

_____

_____

_____

_____

_____

_____

_____

_____

_____

_____

EXERCISE: The Interactional Contract

What are your individual goals?

_____

_____

_____

_____

_____

_____

How do you fulfil these goals? List how you fulfill your individual goals.

_____

_____

_____

_____

_____

How do feel your partner helps you to fulfill your individual goals?

_____

_____

_____

_____

_____

What are your relationship goals?

_____

_____

_____

_____

_____

_____

Now list how you fulfill your relationship goals.

_____

_____

_____

_____

_____

How do you feel your partner helps to fulfill your relationship goals?

_____

_____

_____

_____

_____

What do you think are your partner's individual goals?

_____

_____

_____

_____

_____

What do you think your partner's relationship goals are?

_____

_____

_____

_____

_____

Now list how you help to fulfill your partner's goals.

_____

_____

_____

_____

_____

What could your partner do that s/he is not presently doing that would be helpful to you.

_____

_____

_____

_____

_____

_____

What could you do for your partner that you presently are not doing that would be helpful to him/her? Please be as specific as you can.

Now ask your partner to fill out the same form and compare lists. See if both of you knew each other's individual and relationship goals. If not, adjust your lists to correct depict each other's goals.

This list can be done in the present or it can be used to specify a "five year relationship plan," which would then list goals, both individual and relationship, that could be planned for the next five years.

34 WHICH MARRIAGE TYPE ARE YOU?

Attempts to classify couple partners have been organized into rough groupings. Some groupings are based on individual dynamics, others on conflict and power dimensions, and still others on broad types of "normal" relationships in the marriage. They are helpful only in the sense that you will see that there are many different couple types and that couples engage in many different behavioral profiles. So while you may find similarities between your own behavior and the behavioral profile, in most cases, most couples represent a mix of more than one type.

Couple therapist Clifford Sager describes seven "behavioral "profiles" of couples. These consist of ways that couple partners have of relating to their mate. Such behavioral profiles are not fixed and rigid; most partners may manifest characteristics from different profiles or may move from one pattern to another within a given day. The determinants of the profiles are multi-causal and cannot be precisely explained on the basis of present knowledge. These profiles, according to Sager, are not necessarily how persons think they behave or what they think they want, but how they actually behave. Although the profiles require more research testing, he believes that they have considerable clinical value. Essentially, they provide a kind of organizing schema for observing couple behaviors and transactions.

The following are the seven behavioral profiles or partner types:

Equal Partners

> *George and Mary agreed before marriage that she would keep her career. Actually it was a necessity since they wanted to save up for a house. Although they both wanted to eventually have children, Mary was quite certain that after children were born, they would hire a baby-sitter to care for them while she continued to work outside of the home. Although somewhat reluctant at first, George finally agreed. When they set up housekeeping, their roles were allocated in a flip-flop way. This means that whoever was around when something needed to be done did it. If the dishes needed to be washed and Mary had an appointment with a client and had to leave after dinner,*

> *George cleaned up. If Mary was home earlier than George, she started dinner. This arrangement occurred quite naturally; they really didn't have to discuss it at all. And it worked for them. They both knew how to take care of everything around the house.*

The equal partner wants equality for self and partner. He or she tends to be cooperative and independent. An equal partner is capable of sustained intimacy without clinging and is able to share or assume decision-making and to allow the mate to do the same. An equal partner gives and accepts love. He or she is relatively free of infantile needs that must immediately be fulfilled. Furthermore, he or she does not believe that his or her loveability depends on skillfulness in fulfilling the infantile needs of a mate. At appropriate times the equal partner can be either parental or childlike but is not "stuck" in either position. This person behaves as an equal partner in couple interaction and desires an equal relationship (whether or not the partner has the same desire for equality).

Romantic Partners.

> *Lou and Lisa married after six months of an intense courtship. In many ways, they seemed to be an ideal couple. Both were nice looking; both had good jobs; both had the same aspirations for their life together. In many ways, they were the envy of their friends. Sometimes when they would go out with friends, their friends would call the next day complaining that they had an argument with their partner because their partner asked, "Why can't you be more like Lou or Lisa?" This happened because when Lou and Lisa were together, they were always touching each other, or kissing each other. They were very attentive to each other's moods and needs. They were always sending each other cards, flowers, or little mementos to express their love. Sometimes Lou would call Lisa in the middle of the day and tell her they were both taking off work the next day and going sailing.*

The romantic partner is dependent on a mate. He or she feels incomplete without a partner. Sentiment and anniversaries are extremely important. Such a partner is likely to be possessive and controlling, and is vulnerable if the partner refuses to play a reciprocal role. The partner must be a soul mate with similar reactions and values. Great value is placed on the intensity of love and the passion of sex as criteria for the relationship's success. Two romantic partners can be a very successful couple. A romantic partner in combination with an equal partner may create problems in the marriage if the romantic partner pushes for a great deal of togetherness and exclusivity. This person acts as if he or she is incomplete and requires a romantic partner in order to be whole.

Parental Partners.

> *Alex and Eva have been married for about ten years. Basically their relationship is a good one—at least in terms of day-to-day living. Alex tells Eva what to do and she does it. She sort of likes it that way—she doesn't have to worry about any of the major decisions. Alex takes care of everything. He bought the house and then took her to see it; he purchased their latest car and then drove it home. He says she doesn't have to worry her sweet little head about these things. She has more important things to worry about like what to cook for dinner and what to wear to their dinner party Saturday night. Sometimes, Eva wishes that Alex would take her opinion into consideration but basically she feels he is smarter than she is.*

A parental partner relates to the mate as to a child. Behavior may range from very controlling and authoritative to mildly patronizing. It may be benign and rewarding or assure the parental partner that he or she is needed and is therefore "loved." Torvald in Ibsen's The Doll House" is the prototype, as the early Nora is the prototypic childlike partner. Particularly relevant is one subtype of the parental partner known as the "rescuer" who Infrequently teams up with a "save me."

This type involves a master (essentially an authoritarian and controlling parent stance carried to an extreme.). It includes a rescuer subtype who typically establishes a temporary complementary relationship with a "save me" type during a crisis. This partnership is relatively unstable and a transient one that often begins to crumble after the rescue is over.

Childlike Partners

> *Ronnie and Beth have been married eight years. Visiting them is like going on a roller coaster. You have to prepare yourself for the excitement before you actually get there. When you go into their home, you never know what you will encounter. It could Ron up in the top of a tree, building a tree house for their two-year-old son or Beth baking twenty strawberry short cakes because she was in the mood. They tend not to think too far in advance and sometimes suffer from unintended consequences like when Ron played a joke on his boss and almost got fired. They seem happy together but when you go to visit them, you can't stay there too long without feeling anxious. You never quite know what will happen at any given moment. Their kids probably feel that way also.*

This partner complements the parental partner. The childlike partner seems to encounter the most difficulty when competing with children for care and attention. These partners may find the presence of children threatening to their position with the new partner, and could become unable to meet the children's needs for parenting. Childlike-childlike partnerships, the "sandbox marriage," can function over a short range but are unstable in the long run. Crises develop and each partner wants the other to be the parent, but neither accepts the parental role.

This is basically a profile of a person who wishes to be taken care of, but who actually may wield the power in the couple relationship. The counterpart of the parental profile, this person exhibits the "save me" subtype mentioned above.

The Rational Partner

Bea and Ray always approached decision making in a rational way. They both hated surprises and liked knowing how and when things were going to happen — exactly. Like when they had their first child. When they learned that Bea was pregnant, an event that was completely planned, they set about developing a just and fair schedule for the caretaking of their yet unborn child. Bea would attend to the baby on odd days and Ray would do the caretaking on even days. If the odd days outnumbered the even days for a particular year, then Ray would owe Bea the extra time. This could be paid back on a pay back system—with Ray trading Bea for household chores until his "tab" was paid up. Their plan worked smoothly until one day when Seth, their now three-year-old child, fell off the kitchen chair. Both Bea and Ray looked at their watch to see whose turn it was to caretake, since on that day Ray was paying Bea back from 7PM until 8PM.

The rational partner tries to establish a reasoned, logical, well-ordered relationship with responsibilities of partners well defined. He or she forms a close and emotionally dependent relationship but cannot see that emotions influence behavior. This partner is often more dependent than he or she appears to be. Underneath the rational partner's logic, there are genuine feelings of closeness and affection for the mate, as compared with the parallel partner who may be emotionally out of touch with the partner. The rational partner's sense of order can be positive in marriage, but s/he may also find the complexity and fluidity difficult to take. We often see that such partners are confused and at odds with their children's responses to their approach. The rational partner often acts as a steadying sail for a more volatile one, while the latter serves a the first partner's emotion expressor, one whom the rational partner can gently censure for going too far or being too enthusiastic when the rational partner's anxiety is aroused.

This type is strongly defended against admitting that emotions may affect her or his actions and tries to form a logical, orderly relationship with the partner.

Companionate Partners

> *Rich and Ginny were married now for twenty-two years. Most of their marriage was spent around doing things they both enjoyed with their two boys. While theirs was not a passionate marriage, they both liked spending time with each other— but not too much time. Both of them liked their own space also. When they made love, it wasn't too often and wasn't too romantic but they both agreed that it was comforting. They knew they would always be married and felt very comfortable and secure in their relationship, unlike some of their friends who argued and disagreed over even the smallest issue. Rich and Ginny were glad that they were friends.*

The companionate partner seeks to ward off loneliness and to establish a relationship that need not include romantic love or passion but does include thoughtfulness, loyalty, and kindness given to, and desired from, the partner. The companionate partner wants married life, but may be afraid to love again. When love is demanded there can be problems. Often companionate partners will carefully work out financial agreements and other arrangements for a second marriage. Problems arise at times from a tendency to live with too many idealizations of marriage. Although it often starts as a marriage of convenience and accommodation, the companionate marriage can blossom into a very gratifying relationship for both partners. The basic wish of this type is a partner with whom to share daily living. A person of this type exhibits behaviors that are aimed at escaping being alone. This type typically can tolerate closeness.

Parallel Partners

Mathew and Nikki are both in their late thirties. Married for twelve years, they have basically worked things out between them. Mathew is a successful caterer and Nikki is a salesperson in a boutique. Both love their jobs and spend a lot of time working. Even when they're home, they spend time working. When they aren't working, they do leisure activities. Mathew loves golf and Nikki does aerobics. On the weekends, when he isn't working, Mathew is often playing golf on both Saturday and Sunday. Nikki, always busy, is either off doing aerobics or shopping with her friends. Sometimes they say they never see each other. When this happens they decide to make a "date" with each other. Usually this works but occasionally they even wind up breaking their date! Actually, they mainly communicate through the notes they leave each other on the refrigerator. They seem happy but sometimes they feel they're living separate lives.

This marriage is that of parallel partners. The parallel partner interacts with his/her mate to avoid an intimate relationship. S/he desires distance and emotional space yet maintains all the forms of an intimate home. But emotionally this is not close. The partner's lives run parallel, rather than intertwined. His or her need to maintain distance usually stems from a fear of becoming merged with and controlled by a partner. If the partners get too close, they may feel invaded by his/her partner. Avoiding an intimate relationship is the goal of this type's behaviors. The partner is expected to accept the independence and emotional distance that such a couple relationship entails.

Sager describes a large number of partnership combinations that may be found, such as the equal-romantic, romantic-rational, partner-partner, childlike-childlike, and others.

The typology does not attempt to note the degree of conflict, the positive or negative complementarity, or the motivation of the couple. In most instances there is a second set of profiles that emerges under certain conditions. It is this second set, along with the complementarity, that often makes it possible for a marriage to survive that otherwise would not. Behavioral profiles can and do change. The therapist helps the couple find better adaptations for fulfilling their goals and clears the way for changing some terms in the marriage contract to arrive at a single one that both partners can agree upon.

35

COUPLE STYLES

Perhaps the most widely known and accepted classification of marriages is based on a study by John Cuber and Peggy Harroff of more than 400 couples who had been married for more than ten years and had never seriously considered divorce. These researchers classified the couples into one or more of the following types:

- **The Conflict Habituated**
- **The Devitalized**
- **The Passive-Congenial**
- **The Vital**
- **The Total**

From their study, they developed a typology of couple relationships that depicts the modal kinds and quality of interaction that may be present in marriage. These types are not indicative of couple adjustment since even those couples that are conflict habituated are adjusted to such a style and climate of interaction. Conflict habituated, devitalized, passive-congenial, vital, and total are merely labels that are probably representative of styles and climates of interaction that may pervade any marriage.

The Conflict-Habituated Marriage
In this type of husband-wife configuration, there is much tension and conflict, although largely controlled. At worst, there is some private quarreling, nagging, and bringing up of the past of which members of the immediate family, and more rarely even close friends and relatives have some awareness. At best, the couple is discreet and polite, genteel about it when in the company of others, but rarely succeeds completely in concealing it from the children, although they believe that that they do. The essence however is that there is awareness by both husband and wife that Incompatibility is pervasive. Conflict is ever-potential and an atmosphere of equilibrated tension permeates their lives together. These relationships are sometimes said to be dead or over but there is a more subtle valence here— a very active one. So central is the necessity for channeling conflict and bridling hostility that these imperatives structure the togetherness. In other words, the conflict is the glue that holds the marriage together.

Some psychiatrists have gone so far as to suggest that it is precisely the conflict and the habituated need to do psychological battle with one another, which constitutes the cohesive factor, which ensures continuity of marriage. Possibly so, but from a less psychiatric point of view, the overt and manifest fact of habituated attention to handling tension, keeping it chained and concealing it, becomes the overriding life force. And it can and does for some, last a lifetime. This type of marriage is characterized by constant disagreements and quarreling. While most of us would probably find such a couple relationship intolerable, these couples apparently thrive on the conflict and verbal skirmishes. In fact, it is the stimulation provided by the continual conflict that presumably holds the marriages together, often aided by the satisfactory sex life. In short, the couple constantly fight yet does not break up. They remain together because they somehow find the conflict and fighting rewarding.

There are usually attempts to conceal the true intensity of conflict from friends, relatives, and children. Even so, concealment is seldom successful. They found that incompatibility is pervasive, that conflict is ever potential, and that an atmosphere of tension pervades the togetherness." In this type of relationship, participating in, yet attempting to control, the level of tension and conflict become dominant activities of the husband and wife. They suggest that these couples may need conflict at a psychological level, and that the tension and conflict are the cohesive forces that hold the couple together, even for a lifetime.

Often such discordant couple patterns are based on provocations, in which both partners do or say things that they know will annoy the other, as if they receive satisfaction from keeping things stirred up. In any event, for better or for worse, they create their own unique pattern of communication/interaction as well as the intimate and quality of their marriage.

The Devitalized Marriage
In the Devitalized Marriage, the couples once had a close relationship and a loving relationship, including a fulfilling sex life, but have drifted into an "emotional divorce" and empty marriage. This second type of

relationship is described as "exceedingly common." Sex has become a minor part of married life, little time is spent together because each has different and separate commitments, and the time spent together is viewed by each as his or her duty. Here the relationship is essentially devoid of zest. There is typically no serious tension or conflict and there may be aspects of the marriage which are actively satisfying, such as mutual interest in children, property, or family tradition. But the interplay between the pair is apathetic, lifeless. There is no serious threat to the marriage. It will likely continue indefinitely, despite its numbness. It continues, and conflict does not occur because of the inertia of the "habit trap." Continuity is further insured by the absence of any engaging alternatives, all things considered. Perpetuation is also reinforced, sometimes rather decisively, by legal and ecclesiastical requirements and expectations. These people quickly explain that there are other things in life, which are worthy of sustained human effort. But the relationship between the pair is essentially devoid of vital meaning, essentially empty, by comparison to what it was when the mating began and what was considered to be its raison d'etre.

This kind of relationship is exceedingly common. Many persons in this category do not accurately appraise their position because they frequently make comparisons with other pairs, many of whom are similar to themselves. This fosters the illusion that "this is the way marriage is."

While these relationships lack vitality, there is something there. There are occasional periods of sharing at least something, if only a memory. Formalities can have meanings. Anniversaries can be celebrated, even if a little grimly, for what they once commemorated. As one said, "Tomorrow we are celebrating the anniversary of our anniversary." Even clearly substandard sexual expression is said by some to be better than nothing, or better than a clandestine substitute. A good man or good mother for the kids may with a little affection and occasional companionship now and then get you by.

But even though the couple feels little more than indifference toward each other and has an unsatisfactory sex life, they somehow get along and maintain the marriage. Many undoubtedly consider it natural for marriage to become dull and routine after the romantic excitement and unrealistic highs of the earlier months and years of marriage have passed.

Cuber and Harroff have concluded that the devitalized marriage is probably the most common type in our society and with time it is highly vulnerable to dissolution. They describe it as, on the subjective, emotional dimension, the relationship has become apathetic, lifeless; however, no serious threat to the continuity of the marriage is generally acknowledged. It is intended, usually by both, that it continue indefinitely, despite its numbness.

The Passive-Congenial Marriage

The Passive-Congenial marriage differs from the devitalized in that the partners never had anything but an empty relationship to begin with and hence experience no sense of having lost an exciting and satisfying relationship. The passivity, which pervades the association, has been there from the start. There are two routes by which people make their way into the passive-congenial mode of interaction— either by default or by intention. There is so little that they have cared about deeply in each other that a passive relationship is sufficient to express it all. In other instances, the passive-congenial model is a deliberately intended arrangement for two people whose interests and creative energies are directed elsewhere than toward the pairing— either into careers or into children or community activities. They say they know this and want it this way. These people simply do not wish to invest their total emotional involvement and creative effort in the male-female relationship. Often the marriage is one of convenience, and the couple remain together because of inertia, children, community standing, or financial considerations.

This configuration seems roughly about as prevalent as the preceding one. There is little suggestion of disillusionment or compulsion to make believe to anyone. Existing modes of association are comfortable to adequate— no stronger words fit the facts. There is little conflict. They tip-toe rather gingerly over and around a residue of subtle resentments and frustrations. In their better moods they remind us that there are many common interests, which they both enjoy. When they get specific about these common interests, it typically comes out that the interests are neither very vital things nor do they involve participation and sharings which could not almost as ell be carried out in one sex associations or with comparative strangers. We both like classical music. We agree completely on religious and political matters. We both love the country and our eccentric neighbors or we are both lawyers.

We get the strong feeling when talking with these couples that they would have said the same things when they first married- or even before. When discussing their decision to marry, some of them gave the same rationales for that decision that they do now for their present relationship, some twenty or thirty years later. This is why we have said that they seem to be passively content, not disillusioned even though, as compared to the next type, they show so little vitality and so little evidence that the partner is important- much less indispensable- to the satisfactions, which they say, they enjoy.

Many enter such marriages in a calculating and unemotional way. While the lack of emotional involvement typically results in less conflict, the marriage is also less satisfying. The partners are resigned rather than committed to each other.

The Vital Marriage
The Vital Marriage is a relatively ideal type of warm, loving relationship in which the partners are intensely interested in and committed to their relationship. This type of interaction is found in only a minority of marriages. The vital couple is like most other couples: they argue, disagree, occasionally engage in conflict, but in all negative confrontations there is a willingness and a commitment to forgive and forget. The essence of the vital relationship is that the mates are intensely bound together psychologically in important life matters. Their sharing and their togetherness is genuine. It provides the life essence for both man and woman. This does not mean that they agree on or share in everything. Rather the vital couple

relationship is one in which the partners have reached a virtually total consensus on what is mutually important. They then have reached a mutual agreement to attack these areas with vigor and together. They are not locked into restrictive togetherness, and each is given room for autonomy and personal growth. At the same time they engage in a great deal of mutuality and sharing. They place a premium on open communication and the quick resolution of conflicts. Chronic conflicts are rare. Most couples in vital marriages consider sex an important and pleasurable component, and the partners work at achieving sexual compatibility.

Partners in vital relationships tend to possess personality traits that foster (a) otherness rather than selfness, (b) sexual expressiveness, (c) determination, (e) and high ego strength or stress tolerance. The greatest danger to vital marriages stems from failure to balance individuality and mutuality (separateness and togetherness) for either extreme represents a serious danger to the relationship.

It is hard to escape the word vitality here—vibrant and exciting sharing some of the important life experiences. Sex immediately comes to mind, but the vitality need not surround the sexual focus or any aspect of it. It may emanate from work, association in some creative enterprise, child rearing, or even hobby participation. The clue that the relationship is vital and significant derives from the feelings of importance about it and that the importance is shared. Other things are readily sacrificed for it. It is apparent, even sometimes to the superficial observer, that these people are living for something which is exciting; it consumes their interest and effort, and the particular man and woman who shares it is the indispensable ingredient in the meaning which it has.

The Total Marriage
The Total Marriage is similar to the vital but has more facets. Not only is the relationship a close and loving one, characterized by open communication and effective conflict resolution, but also the process of sharing is even more strongly emphasized. There is a minimum of conflict and of private experience. Even business deals

and professional activities are worked out together. Couples in such marriages may operate a store together, or write books together, or otherwise intertwine their professional and personal lives.

The total marriage relationship is a vital relationship and more. Couples in this last type of couple interaction are totally meshed in interests, tastes, needs, and role performances. They spend all of their time together, reveling in each other's company. The two have become in essence one- separate yet together, individuals yet de-individualized. It goes without saying that although many have a total relationship as an ideal goal, most couples never attain and maintain such a state of couple perfection. For those who do, the bliss is obvious.

Relationships are not made vital much less total by asserting them to be so, or by deceiving the neighbors that they are so. This is not to deny that the total relationship is particularly precarious precisely because it is multifaceted, it is multi-vulnerable as circumstances change.

The total marriage is rare as is the vital marriage. The majority of marriages range from conflict habituated to passive congenial.

Because marriage is subject to change over time, marriages may shift from one style to another. Furthermore, each type of marriage may be based on a traditional or egalitarian marriage script. Understanding the differences between marriage types may be helpful in planning the type of relationship you want and in working toward its achievement. It can also help those of you who are already married better understand the type of marriage you have established. In developing a marriage, partners can create their own heaven or hell, or perhaps their own purgatory.

A Note On Couple Classification

None of the approaches to classifying marriages is perfect. Those made by researchers have their values and their limitations. One of their strengths is that they give the couple a sense of perspective about marriages and sometimes call attention that might otherwise be overlooked. Classifications made by academicians sometimes seem abstract and over simplistic. Hence they may apply to many couples to a limited degree but not fit a particular couple to the extent that they appear realistic and helpful for practical interventions.

The typologies and characterizations have the value of being useful for dealing with the particular couple that is being described. On the other hand, the descriptions may be too limited and may not allow for differences so that they can be applied to other couples.

All of this would seem to support the idea that the reader should carefully select their particular conditions and needs of the particular couple types listed. General categories and classificatory schemes certainly have value, since applying general concepts to couples may provide successful outcomes in some instances.

EXERCISE: Couple Types

Using the Seven Couple Types listed earlier decide which type you
are and why.

_____

_____

_____

_____

Then decide which type your partner is and list why.

_____

_____

_____

_____

Working alone, decide which type you would like to be and what you
could do to accomplish it. Ask your partner to do the same.

_____

_____

_____

_____

Then, together decide which relationship type you would like to
be and negotiate the differences. Then give your couple type a new
name, in this sense, you are creating a unique, special relationship

type that all of your own. Next list what each of you could do to accomplish the relationship type that you want.

_____

_____

_____

_____

_____

_____

_____

_____

_____

_____

_____

_____

_____

_____

_____

_____

_____

_____

36

COMMUNICATION STYLES

It is a truism that happily married couples are able to talk to one another more effectively than unhappily married couples can. They have fewer problems and they deal with those problems more effectively.

Surprisingly, rather little research has been done either on the improvement of communication in marriage or on the different styles of communication that married couples use. Birchler found that happily married couples are much more positive in their behaviors toward their mates. They cooperate more, compromise more, and say "please" and "thank you" more. Interestingly, the unhappy couples, when paired with persons other than their partners in the laboratory situation, also become much more positive in their behaviors: they listened better, smiled more, and interrupted less.

There Are Basic Communication Styles:

Complementary
In this style, each partner serves as a counterpoint to the other. For example, one may do all the talking while the other does all the listening. If both partners were to speak at the same time, they would be competing with each other for center stage. So if A is speaking, B listens. When B is speaking, A listens. If A shouts, B is quiet and so forth.

Conventional
In this type of communication, the couple maintains a casual, light, friendly, chatty conversation to avoid the real issues. They talk about the "weather" etc. which serves to maintain their relationship while maintaining ignorance of the unique and private views of the speakers.

Speculative
This style is directed toward exploring the facets of an issue or problem. The speaker expresses tentative beliefs and ideas about the topic and waits respectfully to hear the opinions of his or her partner. This is an analytical style that emphasizes facts and problem solving rather than disclosure of feelings. For example, "So, is it that you get

upset when I come home late or is it that I don't call when I'm coming home late? Or, it seems to me that one reason for my forgetting to call is that I'm too preoccupied with this new contract at work. Do you see this as a possibility or do you think other things are going on?"

Controlling

In this style, the intent is to persuade or to issue directions, thereby modifying or controlling the partner's behavior. The person's speech is usually sprinkled with, "you should, you ought," and unsolicited pieces of advice. This style is high in self-disclosure of beliefs and feelings and tends to suppress contradictory beliefs and feelings in the partner. "You should not come home late and if you must, only if you must, than you should call."

Contactful

Here, the intent is to share feelings and ideas. It is characterized by the speaker's willingness to express thoughts and feelings openly and to solicit and respectfully listen to those of the partner. Contactful communication is explicit, responsive, and accepting and involves a high degree of disclosure.

Communications can also be flexible (adapting to changes in the ongoing interaction), rewarding (conveying acceptance, appreciation, and support), or aversive (conveying negative personal messages). "I feel sad when I come home late and I see that you are disappointed. It reminds me of the time when I forgot to buy my Mom a birthday card for her birthday. I felt so bad."

37

EARLY WARNING SIGNS AND COMMUNICATION HINTS

> *Sal and Gloria were married for twenty-one years. They had two sons who were presently away at college. They were married quite young and when Gloria initiated counseling; they were both in their early forties. It was already too late. Their marriage was over. Sal had informed Gloria the week before that he was leaving her and that he had been involved in a long term extra couple affair for the past six years. Gloria was shocked! She had absolutely no idea. When asked if there were any signs of his distancing in the couple relationship, she strongly replied that there were not. He never went out in the evening. He was very predictable. Their sex life was the same as it always had been. He was involved in family life and seemed to be concerned about her and the children.*

This situation is a common one—a marriage that seems stable; a relationship that appears committed; a partner that tends to be predictably positively involved. Then, one day, seemingly out of the clear blue, one of them informs the other that the marriage is over and has been for a very long time. The other partner is shocked—had no idea that this was about to occur. When asked if there were signs, he or she invariably replies, "No."

Generally, when couples come for marriage counseling, they have already experienced a great deal of pain and their marriage is often at risk. Among some of the more typical presenting problems are alcohol or drug abuse, sexual dysfunction, partner abuse (physical or emotional), continual conflict, and /or extra couple relationships.

These though are <u>not</u> the kinds of situations we wish to address in this section. Rather, the issues we wish to explore are more insidious and generally more common in couple relationships. We are more interested in the early pre-conditions of couple risk, those events that can act as danger signals to couples that are functioning quite well. We are interested in couple slippage—the manifestations, the signals (both emotional and behavioral), and the curative strategies that couples can employ to reenergize their marriage and/or to reduce the chances of further slippage.

Manifestations of couple slippage generally fall into 10 broad categories: negating the perceptions of the partner, sarcastic teasing, frequent disagreement over minor issues, sexual and/or couple apathy, need for validation by others, predictable cycles or lack of romance in the marriage, spousal irritations, communication problems, a "thing" coming between them, and jealousy.

1. Negating The Perceptions

This occurs when one partner views an event differently and one partner cannot tolerate any viewpoint other than his/her own. In other words, there is a rule which states that whatever A says, B must discount it. For example, birthdays were always important to Mary M. When she was a child, her parents lavished her with presents and she always had a big birthday celebration. John M., on the other hand, came from a very large family who rarely celebrated holidays. Birthdays were considered "just another day." So the first time John did not send Mary a birthday card, she felt that he did not love her anymore. Her couple expectations were not met and she was disappointed. He thought she was making a fuss over nothing. Ultimately, this problem could have the potential of becoming a major source of difficulty in the marriage. Remaining unchecked, it could even possibly destroy the marriage because eventually the intolerance of differing viewpoints would increase. Generally, the need for a partner to deny differing viewpoints occurs for one of three reasons: It represents: (1) a learned way of dealing with others which has been acquired through one's family of origin experiences, (2) a power or control issue, or (3) the reluctance to take responsibility for one's actions.

2. Sarcastic Teasing

This is often a flirtation with disaster in disguise. Harmless little love pats soon grow into little digs. The little digs, fueled by feelings of hurt and indignation, can lead to major battles. The first time Sally L. teased Walter L. about his cold-fish behavior in bed, he laughed it off as a minor annoyance. When she said it three months later in front of his friends from work, he was more than mildly annoyed. He soon started to become sensitized to any negative remarks that she made, interpreting them as criticism. Being in a supposedly loving and caring relationship for Walter soon became an experience based on his capacity to tolerate Sally's hostile and derogatory remarks.

3. Arguments

All couples experience minor disagreements. In and of themselves, arguments generally are not problematic for relationships. They happen on a fairly regular basis, are resolved and forgotten. However, if they begin to increase in number and/or intensity, or if the same issues keep cropping up remaining unresolved, then they could signal a slippage in the relationship. Frequent arguments could also signal what is called the pursuer-distancer theme. The couple is comfortable with a certain level of intimacy. Once their closeness increases, they both become uncomfortable. Arguing with each other creates distance, serving to bring them back to a more comfortable level of intimacy. The distancing effect of constant bickering produces a frustration and self-defeating cycle, such that, when one partner seeks greater distance from the other, then the other is stimulated to react by seeking greater closeness with the distancing partner, who now in turn must seek even greater distance. This cycle ends when the "cat and mouse" game exceeds the tolerance level of either partner and derails the relationship. Bruce M. constantly sexually pursued Susan M. She rejected him on a regular basis. During therapy, it was suggested that Bruce stop approaching Susan and that Susan would approach him sexually when she was interested. This resulted in a much greater response on Susan's part; however, it did not solve the problem because when Susan began approaching Bruce, he rejected her. The real issues were fears of intimacy, vulnerability, and engulfment.

4. Sexual Apathy

Sexual apathy or a change in sexual patterns may reflect early couple slippage. Sexual apathy may reflect a partner's fear of intimacy/rejection or may be a form of payback. In the first case, when a partner fears intimacy/rejection, the lack of sexual interest may serve as a way of avoiding closeness or being rejected. In the second case, rejection of the others' sexual needs, along with one's own, often is a partner's attempt to compensate for feelings of powerlessness and hurt in another area of the relationship. It is a way of paying the other back or of gaining "bargaining chips" in an ongoing struggle to manipulate the other's behavior.

Couples often use the sexual arena to act out problems they are having in the non-sexual areas of their relationship. Dianne M. and Ron M. came for therapy because Dianne would not have sex with Ron. At first glance it appeared that she did not like sex, receiving no gratification or pleasure. Closer examination revealed that she felt powerless in the marriage, with Ron controlling all finances and making all major and minor decisions. As a result she felt unimportant and insignificant. Refusing to have sex with him was one area in their relationship that she could control. Thus, the couple conflict expanded to the bedroom.

5. Seeking Others' Approval

Validation through the other is similar to problem number one in that it represents the flip side of the coin. Whereas number one involves the consistent negation of alternate values; validation through other involves an acceptance of all of a partner's values. Here one partner continuously seeks the other's approval or help and in so doing is extremely sensitive to the other's disapproval or lack of enthusiasm. In this situation the individual's self worth is determined by the opinions and behavior of the other partner. Both problems involve identity issues in that one person's sense of identity is determined by either negating or accepting the other's frame of reference. Colleen L. was raised in a strict Catholic home. Coming from a large family, her behavior was kept under strict control by her parents and older siblings. When she married Jim, she devoted her entire life to being a good wife and mother. Her identity was determined by him in that all of her interests and time were scheduled around his needs. The slightest hint of criticism from him devastated her. Once her feelings were hurt, he then had to spend enormous amounts of time consoling her before she felt calmed.

6. Negative Patterns

Predictable cycles in marriage refer to repetitive patterns that do not have positive outcomes. They are often played out by one partner's actions producing as strong a reaction in the other, which then touches off an even stronger reaction in the first partner. Each reaction is stronger than the previous one. The couple becomes stuck in this vicious cycle. The rule here is that A must say something a little worse than what B just said (x+1). This creates a very predictable yet escalating cycle. The process usually does not end until they frighten each other, either by resorting to physical violence or by devastating each other with words.

When dating, Richie and Samantha showered each other with compliments. Each would attempt to outdo the other with gifts, cards, expressing their love, and compliments. Shortly after they were married, this pattern, each trying to outdo the other, took a negative shift and the discussions began to escalate in a destructive manner.

7. Small Annoyances

Little irritating things refer to the small annoyances of everyday living. If they become too much of a focus, they can become big bothersome things. Leaving the top off the toothpaste is the often-used example. Representative of the little annoying things mentioned in therapy are: bad breath, body odor, too long toenails, leaving cabinet doors opened, leaving little hairs in the bathroom sink, etc. When a person consistently finds his or her partner's behavior irritating, it usually indicates that something else is upsetting him/her, either about him/her self, the other partner or their relationship. The troubled partner may not be aware of what is bothering him/her, but may focus on a symbolic minor feature of the partner's appearance or behavior. Unless action is taken by either partner to explore what is troubling him/her, it can mushroom into unintelligible and nonsensical blowups, leaving both partners devastated and not knowing what is happening or why.

8. Poor Communications

Poor communications often arise because of one of three difficulties: (1) poor communication skills, (2) inability to express feelings, (3) avoidance of intimacy. A person with poor communication skills has chosen or been trained to be either highly verbal or non-verbal. Two people having different communication styles may be at cross-purposes while talking to each other. When one partner is highly verbal, the other may hesitate becoming involved in any discussion because of the apparent verbal superiority of the other. These problems may manifest in a reluctance to verbalize feelings or needs, leading to frustration and resentment. Lack of awareness, understanding, and appreciation of differences in communication styles can contribute to increasing conflict and feelings of alienation. In other cases, individuals may have difficulty asserting/expressing themselves. This problem is often directly related to a problem of low self-esteem. In other cases, fears of rejection/retaliation may underlie the communication problem. One partner may avoid confrontations or sensitive areas of interactions because s/he fears intimacy or feels reluctant to aggravate the other.

9. Outside Interests
Sometimes, "things" come between a couples. These "things" can be represented by anything or anyone. Some examples are: a job, an interest/hobby, friends, over-functioning in a parent role and under-functioning in the husband/wife role, etc. This could signal either that the marriage is not yet established in a committed way or that it is in the process of deterioration. If this process is allowed to go unattended and unchecked, then couple strife is sure to follow.

10. Jealousy
Jealousy can threaten a marriage. Jealousy is often a preexisting condition for one or both of the partners. It can either be accidentally or deliberately triggered. Jealousy often reflects a person's lack of self-concept in one of two ways. In the first situation, the partner could be expressing the need to possess the other. This is manifested by one trying to control the other's activities or by holding him/her accountable for his/her behavior. In the second situation, the one partner's self concept is in need of constant reassurances. The person needs to be constantly reminded through continued attention that s/

he is loved and therefore okay. This condition often flares up quickly into an intolerable jailer-prisoner scenario.

The above are the major indicators of early couple slippage. Some other indicators are partners spending less time together, unilateral decision making without partner consultation, decline in the use of affectionate nicknames previously used, turning to friends or family of origin for emotional support, unsatisfied requests, and/or decline in or lack of playfulness. Before situations get too far out of hand, there are some very immediate and effective measures that couples can take to address these signs of early couple slippage. Initially, they need to be sensitive to the appearance of these signs. Then, partners need to alert each other to the presence of such signals and request cooperation in the exploration of them. Both partners need to talk about the situation until concerned feelings and perceptions have a favorable resolution. If these initial suggestions are not helpful, then partners need to stop interactions when they begin to deteriorate. These techniques may also facilitate the resolution of early warning signals by placing the couple partners in a better frame of mind. Below are some helpful guidelines which couples can employ to help their communications.

Don't Collect Trading Stamps; Deal With The Issues Immediately. When a person walks away from an interaction without having communicated a need or a feeling, the situation is ripe for "collecting a trading stamp." Years ago, people collected scores of trading stamps to cash them in later for some large prize. Some persons save up petty annoyances, little angry feelings, insecurities, or anxieties to cash them in later for some deeper feeling. The result is usually a major argument. If the small feeling or anxiety had been communicated when it occurred, the result could have led to a resolution with closure and elimination of the negative feeling.

Make Attempts To Reinterpret Negative Perceptions Into More Positive Ones.
What we define as real is based on our past history—experiences, perceptions, etc. All kinds of possibilities exist in any given set of

circumstances, but we can chose which ones to perceive and how to perceive them. This selection process is shaped, molded, and created by us because of our unique psychology and the society in which we live.

Sometimes, because of various socialization factors, one may consistently choose to view himself, herself negatively. Such an individual usually chooses negative statements such as, "She doesn't love me. Why should she? I'm not a worthwhile person." The associated emotional state is depression. Another statement based on negative perceptions of the world in general might be, "He won't like me sexually." The thought is, "Why should he? I'm sure I don't know how to do it right." The associated emotional feeling is anxiety.

We all make such statements at one point or another; at times, they may actually be realistic perceptions. This, however, is not what we are referring to. Our concern here is when the negative perceptions of persons and circumstances are recurring themes or typical patterns— when the person generally chooses to see himself/herself negatively. One step to more positive communication is to restate negative perceptions to include more positive ones. For example, when you are feeling particularly negative about yourself, acknowledge that all possible perceptions exist. Talk to yourself; tell yourself that there are alternatives to the negative definition that you are dwelling on. This kind of healthy thinking involves seeing both negative and positive aspects of yourself. Moving toward positive perceptions, of course, tends to be associated with less guilt, anxieties, fears, and insecurities. Gradually, you can learn to view yourself in a more realistic, comfortable fashion.

Avoid Patterns Of Communication In Which Someone Is A Loser. Aim, Instead, For Two Winners.
Some couples communicate in a way that results in a winner and a loser; someone gains at the expense of the other. This can be called "zero summing." The mindset is, "If one is right, then the other must be wrong," or "If she is right, he must be selfish and inconsiderate." In actuality, this kind of thinking only causes two losers. When this situation exists, the two individuals are off balance. It is always

depressing to be the loser, but in zero-summing situations, the victory of the winner is often shallow and lonely because they've won only at the expense of their partner. To avoid playing the zero summing game, focus on being a team where each helps the other to win but not at the expense of the other.

Free Yourself From Pre-Programmed Responses.

When new responses are made to us, whom we define as negative, we generally exhibit displeasure, almost automatically— in a preprogrammed way. Concentrate on not responding automatically; encourage each other to bracket or suspend and examine initial reactions.

Beware Of Transforming Internal Anxieties About Self Into Critical Attacks On Others.

A common anti-communication technique is the "attack" statement such as, "You're a jerk" or "You're stupid." Often, the true source of frustration with a mate originates out of a sense of failure in oneself.

Let's assume the husband comes home from work and immediately begins yelling at his wife about the condition of the house. He may well be attacking his partner for reasons other than the messy house. He may have performance anxieties about himself in general, and particularly with sex. Perhaps he's concerned about impotence but is psychologically unable to acknowledge this negative fear. It's too threatening for him. With his complaint, he creates a safe situation for himself whereby his wife becomes angry with him and refuses him sex. Then, he doesn't have to worry about performance. His guilt and anxieties are alleviated for the moment, only to return at some later point—probably with more intensity. Acknowledging and communicating negative feelings to the partner could help to rectify the situation.

Avoid Patterns Of Denial/Discounting. Responsibility Shared Is More Rewarding Than Responsibility Denied.

Once a partner has been open enough to communicate an existing problem, it is crucial that the mate not interpret it as a personal affront.

For example, if the husband in the earlier example had communicated his fear of impotence to his wife, she could respond in several ways. She may decide that what he's actually saying has nothing to do with impotence but rather with the fact that he no longer finds her attractive. This makes her a "mind reader," and the honest message from her husband becomes totally discounted; she substitutes what she thinks is the real reason. Now, if she verbalizes this to him, he may attempt to reassure her otherwise. Even at that, the focus has now shifted away from his own anxiety onto reassuring his wife. He must now verbalize his fears again (Probably a painful and unpleasant admission for him) if he's going to establish open communication. A further complication might be that he now becomes hesitant to communicate for fear that the conversation may center on whether or not he thinks his wife is attractive.

Listen And Look. Tune In To Your Partner.
One of the most difficult things for couples to do is to really listen to each other. Oftentimes, we may be listening to someone reporting a situation, an incident, a problem, or a feeling, and we're thinking ahead for something we can say, a similar story we can share which aligns with what they're saying. We're listening, of course, but we're not really hearing what the person is saying. When we use this method of communicating, we lose much valuable information.

One reason why this occurs is that many of us cannot tolerate silence. We feel a constant need to keep the conversation going—silence is something to avoid. What usually occurs is that we are constantly thinking ahead to new topics to bring up while the other is talking. When we exhaust all possible topics, the conversation lapses into what we probably would call boredom.

Enjoy the silence. Relax. Don't feel the need to control or run the conversation. Don't keep talking when there is really nothing left to say. Start Listening. You may even want to create specific periods of calm and reflection when the two of you simply spend time completely alone, undisturbed, yet not "discussing" anything.

Examine And Evaluate Feelings Of Guilt And Anxiety.
There are times when you feel guilty or anxious about certain interactions. Question yourself about where these feelings may be coming from. Have you provided yourself with information so that you can examine the intellectual basis of the negative emotion? Have you communicated the guilt or anxiety in the present so that your partner can respond and thereby help to create closure on the negative emotion? Have you communicated the feeling so that it doesn't intensify over time, so that you don't begin to collect trading stamps? Have you attempted to translate the negative feelings into more positive ones?

Don't be afraid to delve into yourself. Acknowledge the existence of negative perceptions within yourself so that you can take steps to transform them into positive ones.

Open communication provides the basis for couples to trust. Once an individual begins to communicate openly, the groundwork is laid for the mate to reciprocate. When this positive cycle is begun, the couple has the potential for higher levels of satisfaction leading to rewarding intimate awareness.

EXERCISE: Frames Of Reference

Look at one another from varying perspectives. While you're doing these exercises, do not speak with one another. Try to notice the differences between what you see and feel as you vary the closeness and distance and the heights.

For example, look at one another from twenty feet apart. Write down whatever you see and feel.

_____

_____

_____

Now move in closer—say twenty inches apart. Write down what you see and feel.

_____

_____

_____

Now look at each other from varying heights. One should stand on a chair. Both write down what you see and feel.

_____

_____

_____

Now switch and have the other stand on the chair. Write down what you see and feel.

_____

_____

_____

Now make yourselves shoulder to shoulder. Write down what you see and feel.

_____

_____

_____

Next spend time discussing what you each wrote.

_____

_____

_____

_____

_____

_____

_____

_____

EXERCISE: The Closed Fist

Most people are about as happy as they make up their minds to be (Abe Lincoln.)

This exercise will help you to develop awareness about yourself by participating in a symbolic struggle.

Give your partner your tightly closed fist and have him or her try to open it. Then reverse the process.

Answer these questions after you finish the exercise.

What was your struggle like?

_____

_____

_____

What happened? Describe the activity.

_____

_____

_____

_____

What thoughts went through your mind?

_____

_____

_____

_____

What were your strategies?

_____

_____

_____

_____

_____

What feelings developed? And at what point?

_____

_____

_____

_____

_____

How do you feel now?

_____

_____

_____

_____

_____

Does this parallel any other behavior that both of you do?

_____

_____

_____

Below is a Marital Satisfaction Scale. It will indicate to you where the strengths and challenges are in the relationship. First fill out the scale separately. Then discuss your answers.

1. Check on the scale line below which best describes the degree of happiness, everything considered, of your present marriage. The middle point, "happy," represents the degree of happiness which most people get from marriage, and the scale gradually ranges on one side to those few who are very unhappy in marriage, and on the other, to those few who experience extreme joy or felicity in marriage.

0		2	7	15	20	25	35	
.		.	.	.	.	.	.	
Very Unhappy				Happy			Perfectly Happy	

State the approximate extent of agreement or disagreement between you and your mate on the following items.

	Always Agree	Almost Always Agree	Occasionally Disagree	Frequently Disagree	Almost Always Disagree	Always Disagree
2. Handling Family Finances	5	4	3	2	1	0
3. Matters of Recreation	5	4	3	2	1	0
4. Demonstration of Affection	8	6	4	2	1	0
5. Friends	5	4	3	2	1	0
6. Sex Relations	15	12	9	4	1	0
7. Conventionality (right, good, or proper conduct)	5	4	3	2	1	0
8. Philosophy of Life	5	4	3	2	1	0
9. Ways of dealing with in-laws	5	4	3	2	1	0

10. When disagreements arise, they usually result in:

husband giving in, wife giving in, agreement by mutual give and take

0   2   10

11. Do you and your mate engage in outside interests together?

All of them, some of them, very few of them, none of them.

10   8   3   0

12. In leisure time do *you* generally prefer:

to be "on the go," to stay at home

Does your mate generally prefer:

to be "on the go," to stay at home ?

(Stay at home for both, 10 points; "on the go" for both, 3 points; disagreement, 2 points.)

13. Do you ever wish you had not married?

Frequently, occasionally, rarely, never

0   3   8   15

14. If you had your life to live over, do you think you would:

marry the same person, marry a different person, not marry at all

15   0   1

15. Do you confide in your mate:

almost never, rarely, in most things, in everything

0   2   10   10

Scoring:

The scores for all 15 items should be added up together. Higher scores indicate greater satisfaction. This should also point out your strengths and challenges as a couple. This should result in meaningful discussions so that you can enhance your relationship.

38

CONFLICT

Everything that can go wrong will.
(Murphy's Law)

> *He: We met at nine.*
> *She: We met at eight.*
> *He: I was on time.*
> *She: No, you were late.*
> *He: Ah, yes, I remember it well.*
> *(Gigi)*

> *You are like a hurricane*
> *There's calm in your eye*
> *And I'm getting lonely*
> *Some feelings stay*
> *I want to love you*
> *But I'm getting blown away.*
> *(Neil Young)*

The Emergence of Conflict

The incidents that set off conflict more often than not are trivial. The same undercooked eggs that one cheerfully ate before now becomes intolerable. The messy ketchup bottle, the messy bathroom, the lack of enthusiasm for going to the movies or making love --all can produce anger. Often, of course, one's partner is undergoing comparable frustrations and at some point anger meets with anger. Even when a partner doesn't want to quarrel, s/he seldom is prepared to withstand hostile attacks from the other partner. Whenever doubts and/or anxieties surround individuals, the relationship becomes the focus of attention. Without intending to and without wanting to, many young couples test their relationships severely.

Overt Conflict

> *George (calm ... serious) I've got to figure out some new ways to fight you, Martha. Guerrilla tactics, maybe ... internal subversion ... I don't know.*
> *(Edward Albee, Who's Afraid of Virginia Wolf)*

There are many ways to conceptualize conflict. One way is to describe it in terms of acute, progressive, or habituated forms.

Acute conflict is most characteristic of early marriage, and stems from the many undefined situations, which exist then. Its function is to permit the couple to work out a joint pattern of life in which the frustrations that accompany early disillusionment have been worked through. The question of course is whether accommodation will be achieved before quarreling has destroyed the foundation upon which it must rest. As the particular problems that a couple face are resolved, acute conflict tends to disappear from the marriage. It may reappear however, whenever any basic change in conditions produces a new undefined situation. Acute conflict may reappear when the first child is born and continue until techniques for handling the accompanying changes are worked out. Similarly, a promotion, a move to another city, the marriage of one's children, having to care for one's aged parents—all may provoke new outbursts of acute conflict.

Unless couples learn rather quickly to resolve conflict, the probability is great that the conflict will take a directional form; it will become progressive. When acute conflict is not resolved, each quarrel leaves a residue of hard feeling and an area in which the couple cannot communicate very effectively. Then each time a quarrel develops, there is not only the new issue to solve, but the hard feelings and unresolved issues from earlier quarrels as well. The conflict spirals, with the disagreement becoming wider and feelings more bitter. Very much of this may produce estrangement- a condition in which the partners are permanently alienated. Unless the couple is irrevocably committed to the permanence of marriage, movement toward separation and/or divorce may follow.

The tendency for acute conflict to become progressive may explain the large number of marriages, which result in separation during the first year. What is not known is whether marriages that remain intact involve less conflict. It also appears that most intact marriages that survive do show less conflict, and the research seems to show that some intact marriages continue in spite of marked estrangement between the partners.

In the best of marriages there may be little apparent conflict after the initial adjustments are worked out. In the worst of marriages, partner interaction, except for conflict, virtually may not exist. Most marriages probably fall in between. In most areas they have worked out a reasonably satisfactory adjustment, but there also remain areas where they have reached only tentative compromises or where they cannot agree. This may happen in the areas of in-law relationships and money management. In spite of our equal treatment norms, either partner may be unable to accept the in-laws completely. They may avoid contact with them and may lash out at the partner whenever s/he is tactless enough to force the issue. Similarly, after the budget, insurance payments and all of the rest have been worked out; one partner may consistently overspend or underspend as compared to partner's expectations. The situation may generally be kept under control, with open conflict emerging only at a time when the bank statement is received, or when a couple runs out of money before the end of the month.

Such areas of conflict, which crop up again and again, with a stable accommodation never quite being achieved, may be labeled habituated. Habituated conflict differs from acute conflict in that there is not the same emotional investment in it; it is less explosive. In early marriage when a husband sleeps on the living room sofa it may throw his wife into a rage. After a stable adjustment has been made, he may continue to nap on the sofa and his wife may muter with some disgust that he is a lazy slob, but neither he nor she is greatly upset. Habituated conflict also differs from progressive conflict in that it does not become worse. The wife may refer to the husband as a lazy slob, with some overtones of affection.

Covert Conflict

So far we have dealt with couple conflict as though it were synonymous with open fighting. We have assumed that quarreling is normal in marriage as it is in the rest of life and that most couples learn to handle quarreling in marriage as they do elsewhere. To conceive of couple conflict in such limited terms, however, is to miss some of the most significant and devastating ways in which people struggle with each other.

Throughout this book we have assumed that behavior occurs at varying levels of awareness. Some behavior may best be understood as fully conscious and rational. In other instances, people act in ways that do not make sense unless one is willing to assume that certain functions of the behavior are different from the apparent ones. We saw how this operates in dating and mate selection. Now we observe it in marriage.

The pervasiveness of covert conflict in marriage is difficult to estimate. By definition it is hidden and cannot be observed directly. Only through psychotherapeutic evaluation can it often be definitely established. Yet there is widespread agreement that there is a whole series of "emotional withholdings" in many relationships that reveal undercover hostility. Some theorists would say that some conflict is inherent in all relationships and that, if a couple do not at least occasionally disagree openly, one is sure to find evidences of unknowing sabotage in the relationship.

Perhaps the most widely recognized forms of emotional withholding in marriage are in the sexual area. Lack of sexual responsiveness in wives and impotence in husbands are examples. This is not to say that there may not be occasional instances where there are organic problems or there may not be deep-seated psychological factors operating in other cases.

There are other forms of withholding- ways of making one's partner suffer without appearing to do so. The partner who is hypochondriacal often unwittingly uses illness to control the partner and to deny the partner the full joy of living; the ill one must be cared for and catered to, but cannot be expected to be a satisfying sex partner and companion. At less extreme levels, the whole range of psychosomatic illnesses, rashes, allergies, headaches, ulcers, obesity, almost any unexplained symptom- may represent couple conflict.

One problem is that one cannot always be certain that psychosomatic symptoms stem from couple problems. The underlying problems may derive more from conditions at work than at home. They may stem from frustrations encountered outside the home, and they may be tied to problems with parents or children.

Mental health professionals believe that covert conflict is potentially more damaging than is open fighting. When people quarrel, they are at least aware of the problem. The chances are good that the couple will find some sort of solution. When the problem is masked as something else, however, it may take its toll without the difficulty ever being discovered. The loss of efficiency and personal satisfaction stemming from covert conflict may be greater, in some ways, than open conflict, which could lead to couple dissolution.

On the other hand, some marriages may become stabilized around covert conflict. Here, there is the possibility that the personal and social costs of organizing some marriages around an ulcer or migraine headaches may be less than the costs of confronting those couples with the neurotic character of their interaction. Few reasonable people would deny that many ulcerous parents have had outwardly successful marriages and raised apparently healthy, successful children.

39

CONFLICT AND POWER

Several different couple patterns can be grouped under the heading of conflict and power. Couple therapists Lederer and Jackson defined couple power relationships as symmetrical (equal power), complementary (dominant-dominant) and parallel (rule based and varying between symmetrical and complementary). They further described four types of relationships based on the power dimension:

1. **Stable-Satisfactory.** This is where there is explicit agreement about control of specific areas.
2. **Unstable-Satisfactory.** This is where there is temporary, transition during time of change.
3. **Unstable-Unsatisfactory.** This is where there are uncompleted transactions and continued maneuvering for control.
4. **Stable-Unsatisfactory.** This is where there is a withdrawn, cold, pseudo mutual front, with a concealment of instability.

Each of the four types has two subtypes to which Lederer and Jackson gave catchy labels such as the Weary Wranglers and the Heavenly Twins. A key factor in this classification is an exchange of behavior between partners that leads to a relatively workable relationship.

One family therapist has delineated two patterns that couples use in attempts to deal with conflict and relating. One is a centripetal pattern in which the moves are inward and the other centrifugal in which the moves are outward. Those patterns are particularly prevalent among middle aged couples who are dealing with the separation of adolescent offspring from the family.

An example of a centripetal couple is described as a couple pair who shows indications of strain, fatigue, and irritation with each other, but denies to the clinician that there is any problem with the marriage, smiles at each other, and use endearments. It eventually emerges that their sex life is non-existent, but the absence is attributed to work pressures, worries over the children, and bedtime migraine headaches. Such couples express only positive, harmonious, and loving feelings; the tendency is to stick together."

Extreme centrifugal marriages typically end in separation or divorce. Some centrifugal couples remain together "for the sake of the children," who need us," but find their satisfactions outside the marriage. Careers and extra couple affairs rather than the partner tend to claim their respective interests and emotional investments.

These patterns show up in general family functioning as well as in parental handling of adolescents and in the couple interaction. Unlike some of the other classificatory approaches mentioned above, the centrifugal and centripedal patterns are thought to require therapy using what is called a multigenerational treatment approach. For example, the marriage counselor needs to look toward altering the relationships and unresolved issues between the couple partners and their own parents.

EXERCISE: The Sheet of Paper

This exercise will also assist you in discovering your relationship patterns. Take one sheet of paper and pretend that this sheet of paper represents something that both of you want very very much. Using whatever strategies you can, try to get the piece of paper for yourself. You may not rip the paper.

What did you feel when you first saw the piece of paper?

_____

_____

_____

_____

What were the first things that you tried to get the paper from your partner?

_____

_____

_____

What other strategies did you initially try?

_____

_____

_____

What thoughts and feelings did you have about your partner as you were trying to get the paper from him/her and couldn't?

_____

_____

_____

After a while, when you still were unable to get the paper, what strategies or techniques did use to bargain for the paper?

_____

_____

_____

How did you feel about this?

_____

_____

_____

Who eventually wound up with the paper?

_____

How did this eventually happen?

_____

_____

_____

Is this ending typically how power struggles get settled in your relationship?

_____

_____

_____

How could the ending have been different? How could you have negotiated differently?

_____

40

THE PSYCHOLOGICAL TASKS AND TRAPS OF EMOTIONALLY MATURE RELATIONSHIPS

"This is definitely not the man I married! I can't believe this! I can't reach him. He was never like this." Such exclamations are common in couple counseling offices where combinations of shock, dismay, hurt, frustration, and anger are presented, as couples struggle to understand what happened to that blissful time prior to marriage. They ponder how conditions could have so dramatically changed from the time before they were married when they were so in love to the disappointment, hurt, and anger so prevalent in their marriage now. Most couples are hardly prepared for the complexity of processes that are set in motion when the couple contract is sealed. It is most often the first time that the individuals are assuming full responsibility for their own lives, and separating from their primary families of origin to whom strong attachments and dependencies had been formed. The many issues that begin to emerge in the couple union are initially apt to be dismissed with a confident, "We'll work it out. We love each other." In the throes of romantic love and sexual attraction, it is difficult for couples to consider what it is going to be like looking across the breakfast table at their partner day after day. Later, after the negative cycles of interaction are evident and the individuals are worn out from trying to work it out, they present for couple therapy with a sense of failure often stating, "We're unhappy. We can't seem to stop fighting."

It is the purpose of this section to summarize the psychological developmental tasks necessary for the formation of a healthy, stable, long-term relationship. These tasks are explored first before marriage and then in the couple situation. Psychological factors that hinder completion of these developmental tasks are discussed, along with the commonly encountered traps and pitfalls faced by couples who have not completed the tasks.

Pre-relationship Developmental Tasks

Partners in a healthy marriage are continuously changing and growing with respect to their personality development, interests, goals and relationships with friends, relatives, and colleagues. In order for these changes to benefit the couple relationship, flexibility and sensitivity are required on each person's part. This in turn calls for mature skills that will help persons define their partner's psychological growth as a benefit rather than as a threat. Marriage often highlights and intensifies the emotional challenges necessary to achieve greater personal maturity, which in turn, contributes to greater couple happiness. Personal maturity involves the successful negotiation of life tasks that each individual must face. These tasks include: The formation of a positive self-image which allows for spontaneity, curiosity, and more competent intellectual and social skills; b) The separation and independence of the person from their parents into a more self-reliant, and confident individual; c) The development of healthy self-esteem which allows for the expression of love and the ability to give love to others without feeling depleted or deprived; d) The willingness to assume responsibilities and care-taking without feeling resentful or taken advantage of; and e) The capacity to achieve a balance in our personal psychology between reasoning and emotions which allows us to empathize with another's feelings and position.

An emotionally mature relationship requires mutual respect of each partner's growth and changing needs and interests. More mature individuals can adapt to changing dimensions in their partners without feeling rejected, or threatened. They feel comfortable pursuing outside interests and bringing other important people into the couple relationship. Although the capacity to maintain independence in a marriage is most important, the ability to trust and rely on one's partner is an equally vital issue.

More secure individuals, who have come into the marriage after completing the basic developmental tasks, are able to recognize and share fears, insecurities, and limitations. This allows for a reaching out to the partner in times of need, stress, or problems. In this way, both partners feel they are making important contributions to each other, which enhance the feeling of mutual dignity and respectfulness. While this issue of equality and mutual respectfulness may not be emphasized in other cultures, in American society where equality is a significant issue, it is a crucial factor in the smooth functioning of a marriage.

Relationship Developmental Tasks

When one considers the requirements necessary for two married people to remain content through modern day stresses, obligations, and economic, personal, and social pressures, it is important to give and discuss matters which will deeply affect the individual, the partnership, and the eventual family unit.

A successful marriage involves accomplishing fundamental tasks, which we have discussed throughout the book. Some of the more basic developmental tasks are:

- **Continuing to grow as separate individuals in the marriage, while maintaining a working interdependence with society and ourselves. This growth process is what is involved in one's maturing as a person and being respectful of the partner's individuality. It means working out differences in backgrounds, past experiences, and intellectual and personality styles with a spirit of cooperation rather than a power struggle;**
- **Bridging the transition from romantic love to the caring and nurturing involved in a longer term intimate relationship;**
- **Learning to compromise one's own needs with the needs of one's partner so that resentments and feelings of deprivations are held to a minimum;**
- **Mutual agreement on how to allocate household chores so that the workload of marriage and raising a family is equally shared;**
- **The ability to make the transition from the initial romantic phase of the couple relationship to when children are born which brings about important changes in the relationship of the couple;**
- **The effective resolution and management of conflict which is an inevitable accompaniment of a healthy relationship where both partners are express their thoughts, feelings, and needs;**
- **Working to maintain sexual interest so that the couple relationship is the primary relationship in both it's emotional and physical aspects. The couple relationship is one of the most**

significant human experiences, which can foster individual development.

The Role Of Love And Intimacy In Emotionally Mature Relationships

It would be unusual for a couple to maintain the intensity of romantic and erotic feelings that characterize the initial months of marriage. Gradually, the excitement of the relationship is replaced by every day concerns and tasks, which are important to the ongoing maintenance of the relationship. The newness of the sexual experience diminishes, and the conversations that previously revealed interesting information become more directed to practical matters. Hopefully, romantic love transforms into a deeper sense of caring and appreciation as the couple share life situations together, and the coupled bonding becomes a source of friendship, love, and intimacy.

Love

If there is any singular aspect to the feeling commonly described as mature love, it is acceptance. Loving, in its most developed form, involves the embracing of the loved person with a deeper appreciation and approval of that person just as they are. The bonding is cemented by the helpfulness and mutual maturing which each partner renders to the other, with a deepening of appreciation and respectfulness of the other partner's qualities and assets. It is an intuitive understanding and action of extending one's caring feelings to another, without expectations, or judgment, or evaluation. This is a difficult task even for the most mature of couples, for socialization in American society involves being shaped by messages of what is prized and what is valued and what is less worthy of our attention and appreciation. Some individuals learn to be fearful of deeply accepting another because they feel that this might condone ways or qualities of being that are generally disapproved of by society. Furthermore, individuals mistakenly believe that the way to mature and improve themselves is to eliminate what they regard as their undesirable aspects and behaviors. They often are frightened of the process of opening up to, and accepting, aspects of themselves, which they have judged unlovable. They fear that acceptance of these aspects will lead either to stagnation, or to an unwanted redefinition of themselves.

Intimacy

The foundation of intimacy is basic trust and communication. Basic trust is the experience of positiveness toward oneself and those close to us. It allows individuals to feel accepting of themselves and to value their loving feelings. This self-acceptance promotes a more relaxed psychological state of mind, which makes for openness and allows couples to reach out toward each other with positive expectations of returned loving feelings. It diminishes unnecessary protectiveness and anticipation of hurts and rejections. This basic caring feeling toward oneself and others reduces the need to hide behind images, or to feel threatened that unacceptable aspects of ourselves will emerge. Out of this positiveness, communication flows more readily and couples allow themselves to be more "real." Where basic trust is present to a greater degree, partners are more mutually respectful of each other, and unrealistic expectations are minimized. As each partner more readily shares their feelings and difficulties, a better understanding of the needs and capabilities of each partner emerges.

Expectations and idealization of the partner are usually present in the courtship phase of a relationship. These expectations and idealizations derive from unresolved childhood dreams and needs which are then contributed to by one's partner, who is trying to put his/her best foot forward.

As the relationship progresses and each person's idiosyncrasies, problems and limitations become apparent, adjustments to each persons disappointed expectations become vital to sustaining and deepening loving feelings.

As stated earlier, a lasting loving relationship requires the deeper appreciation and acceptance of one's partner as they truly are, not as we expect them to be. This does not mean that if there are significant difficulties and problems that they cannot be addressed and changes hoped for; rather, it means that one starts to work on these problems with patience and an understanding of this is how things are rather than an attitude of, How can you be or act this way? Couple problems can arise when the honeymoon is over, when the partners begin to sense the reality of whom they are with rather than seeing their mates through rose-colored lenses.

Developmental Tasks And Emotional Maturity Or Immaturity
As stated earlier, it is here that the role of individual personality dynamics is important in that they are powerful factors, which relate to the couple's mutual capacity for happiness. It is the degree of nurturance, acceptance, appreciation, and sense of emotional security, which the individuals experienced through their childhood emotional development that will largely contribute to how they respond to their partner over time, and the level of intimacy that they will allow in the relationship. When we speak of levels of maturity, we are in fact, talking about the degree to which the person has been able or encouraged to develop their emotional and intellectual capabilities, along with a stabilized and positive sense of self. When there are blocks to this development such as in childhood situations of abandonment, abuse, neglect, or overindulgence, the person will display troubled personality dynamics.

By personality dynamics we mean the patterned sets of feelings, emotional reactions, and behaviors that people do as a result of their interaction with their environment and significant others. These patternings serve important functions of helping individuals anticipate and manipulate the environment to serve their needs, and to avoid pain, anxiety, or harm.

The human mind and brain functioning is set up in such a way as to shield from consciousness unwanted or painful aspects of feelings, thoughts, and experiences. This does not mean that they are inactive. It simply means that individuals can consciously carry on activities without distraction, more or less, from these unconscious events. This ability carries with it both major advantages and disadvantages. The major advantage is that persons are often spared the immediate pain or discomfort of feelings, which probably helps them to function more effectively in a current, immediate situation.

The major disadvantages are: (1) People are under the illusion that their conscious mental activity is the major source of their decision making and that it represents the major portion of what they would refer to as their mind or personality; (2) They do not understand that there are major aspects of their decisions and behaviors which come from the unconscious reservoir of feelings and rejected aspects of themselves; (3) Feelings which remain unconscious are free to play out in terms of substitute behaviors which are not within awareness, or conscious choice. More importantly, however, the assumptions that are contained within these feeling states are beyond rational assessment. For example, if a young boy has a chronic experience of feeling unworthy because his mother is continuously unhappy, it would not be unusual for the child to blame himself for his mother's unhappiness. If he later goes on to repress this experience, the assumption which he made as a child that he must not have been lovable enough to make his mother happy remains in his unconscious, unquestioned and accepted without reservation. He might therefore respond to the unhappiness in his partner with discomfort and fear, unconsciously feeling that there must be something wrong with him because his wife is experiencing unhappiness and (4) When feelings are unconscious, they posses non-logical properties. For example, parts can stand for wholes, and rules of orderly logic and understanding may not be applicable. The best example of non-logical thinking or feelings is exemplified in dreams. Thus, if an aspect of our partner's behavior reminds us unconsciously of a parent's personality or behavior, it is not uncommon for the piece of behavior to become representative of that individual as a whole, calling forth such reactions as "You're just like my mother!"

While each partner may have entered the marriage with a relatively stable personality, it is a recognized fact that longer-term exposure to a troubled personality of one partner can adversely affect the personality structure of the other partner in important ways. As long as each partner is catering to the needs of the other partner, no matter how maladaptive, the couple will manage to function together and feel that the marriage is viable. As soon as one of the partners seeks a more healthy and permissive environment to develop more of their own personality, there is a significant threat to the relationship (Kaplan and Sadock, 1981). Pressure will be brought to bear on the partner by the less healthy individual to maintain the status quo. This situation is frequently encountered where one partner is alcoholic. Despite the bitter complaints of the sober partner about his/her mate's drinking, s/he nevertheless maintains a control of the relationship, which endows him/her with esteem and power. When the alcoholic enters treatment and begins to make genuine changes in his/her personality and style of interaction, the mate may well sabotage treatment and subtly induce the partner to resume drinking.

Relationship Traps And Pitfalls
There are many pitfalls along the way of the developmental transitions. One would think that being in a "loving relationship" would diminish the anxieties, or the opposite, increase the trust that people experience with one another. This is often not the case, however, as witnessed by the number of partnerships, which deteriorate once the vows of marriage and commitment, are exchanged. One of the main reasons for this is that the intimacy which marriage brings increases the threat of exposure or rejection, which an individual may have feared through his/her life. The more important the partner becomes, the greater the trauma anticipated should s/he be disapproved of or rejected by their partner.

Building Up Protective Mechanisms
The formation of the unconscious and the accompanying defense mechanisms, which serve to protect our mental stability, has been a topic, which has been the basis of concern and exploration of various psychological schools for over the past 50 to 60 years. While various theorists have emphasized feeling components as the basis for forming the need for repression and various defense mechanisms, psychoanalysts tend to agree that the unconscious together with the accompanying defense mechanisms for maintaining repression and

the intactness of the unconscious are important determinants of overt human behavior.

The present auto support the view that one of the most important underlying motivational drives is the need for the individual to maintain a sense of security, low anxiety, and an intact sense of self. This motivational system gives rise to the emphasis on the individual's need for self-protection which easily outweighs conscious considerations of love and romance when the individual feels him/herself to be in any way threatened. It is important to note though. defense or protective mechanisms are not necessarily pathological. If they do not become permanent ways of avoiding reality, they can have adaptive value. If, however, they cause distancing and/or excluding of the partner, they can lead to problems in a long-term relationship.

Individuals' intellectual capacity to reason, anticipate, project, and analyze provides them with powerful tools to adapt and protect themselves. If they are accurate in their appraisal of the current situation and its potential problems or harms, then these processes serve them well. If, however, past wounds and sensitivities cause them to misinterpret present circumstances, then what was a positive asset now becomes a significant limitation, and they are likely to become defensive and emotionally restricted in the face of an anticipated unpleasantness, harm, or rejection. There are significant reasons for how these processes of misinterpretation develop which we will return to, but the main point is that these personality dynamics are crucial in whether the couple relationship will contain greater harmony or greater discord.

Protective measures are built up over a lifetime of experience and become incorporated into an individual's personality makeup. They are experienced by the person as a natural part of themselves, and more importantly, are felt to be a necessary part of their secure functioning. When these protective measures become more extreme, rigid, and inappropriate to the actual threats facing the individual, these defensive measures become maladaptive. Because these protective mechanisms are experienced by the individual as part of him/herself and necessary for survival, they are clung to with the belief that greater harm or threat will come if they are questioned or let go of. Because most of what individuals dislike about themselves and are rejected for by others is in reality their defensive maladaptive maneuvers, they are often in the paradoxical situation of suffering from the very processes they are convinced they need to protect themselves. Indeed, individuals find it difficult to change in spite of their complaints of suffering or rejection until they can experientially understand that the way they are trying to defend against hurt and rejection is the major problem for them.

Painful or emotionally depriving experiences in childhood create a need to compensate for the effects they have had on self-esteem and feelings of self-worth. Individuals then develop expectations of self and others to offset these deprivations and handicaps to self-esteem and set about to fashion a self-image, which excludes what is judged to be undesirable personality features. They long for the acceptance and unconditional love that would have been helpful in the past, and transfer these expectations onto the people who become most important in life. They think, "Surely if I am loved, those who love me will be willing and able to fulfill all my needs and expectations. In this way, they endow their partners with qualities and capabilities to help them accomplish this task only to later become disappointed and angry when they fall short of their expectations. Often, as a result of this process, which may be acted out quite unconsciously, they become angriest and demand the most from those who are closest and most caring.

The need to protect oneself at all costs is most difficult for couples to understand because, for the most part, they are unaware of their underlying feelings. Security measures far outweigh the influence of romantic love which often contains within it idealizations and expectations by one's partner which can be frightening if the other partner is anxious or insecure. In order to avoid being a disappointment, a partner might engage in what may appear to be destructive or unloving behavior, which in reality is defensive, maneuvers to avoid anticipated hurt.

There can be many types and degrees of protective measures invoked, as well as different vulnerabilities, which are triggered by a couple relationship. Much to the puzzlement of many a partner, these protective measures may only appear after a couple has formally entered into a marriage contract. People who have been living together for one to several years and then marry, may find an escalation of conflict in their relationship, which did not exist while they were living together. The reality of a marriage contract, with it's legal, economic, and emotional commitments is often frightening to an insecure partner who may feel trapped, or fearful that s/he will not be able to live up to the expectations of the agreement. S/he might feel the loss of an escape route should something "go wrong" in the relationship or may be frightened that s/he does not have the capacity to sustain a loving relationship. Or, s/he may mourn the loss of the opportunity to still have the option of pursuing other partners as a way of reassuring themselves that they are still desirable.

Another common factor in the formal marriage contract effecting the previously established live-in relationship is the fact that the partner may have held off the expression of strong desires and preferences until s/he felt secure about the commitment. The more anxious partner frequently represses the awareness of these issues until pressured. The formalizing of the relationship then forces that partner to confront issues and feelings, which were kept out of consciousness.

These patterns of behavior, with their attendant needs, expectations, frustrations, disappointments, and disillusionments, are powerful processes because they represent attempts by the person to repair hurts and wounds from childhood. These hurts do not necessarily have to be traumatic events or devastating occurrences. They can be the day-to-day insensitivities and subtle lack of parental responsiveness, which accumulate over time to undercut a child's confidence and positive feelings for life and appreciation of themselves.

While these reparative processes can become maladaptive when they are transferred intact onto a partner, they nevertheless are attempts by that person to repair themselves and calm their inner discomfort. If that positive energy can be harnessed and redirected, then that person has the opportunity to attempt that healing process with different tools.

In evolving defensive mechanisms to protect themselves, just as occurs in the process of worrying, individuals are attempting to anticipate, predict, and thus control a potentially threatening situation. Capacities for anticipation and prediction are dependent on memories of past experiences. When individuals recall past events and project them into the future in anticipation of trying to cope with what they feel is about to happen, they have a sense of power and control. They gear their forces up and feel a certain strength even if it means stirring up and holding onto negative feelings of anger, or hurt. If their estimation of the current situation and its similarity to past experiences is accurate, then the behavior is adaptive. If there are significant inaccuracies or misperceptions either about the present situation or the way things happened in the past, then they are susceptible to maladaptive behaviors.

One of the difficulties in this whole process of adaptation through anticipation and comparison with the past, is that the individual is dealing not only with factual events, but constellations of feelings, some or all of which may be unconscious, which alter the memory or understanding of these events. Therefore, not only are the actual recall of events open to error, but the understanding of the dynamics involved in these events may be faulty. As in our prior example, a mother's chronic unhappiness stemming from an unhappy marriage and personal conflicts can easily be erroneously experienced by a child as resulting from some fault of his in being able to make his mother happy. This set of experiences is then laid down in the child's memory and reproduced in his current feelings as they may apply to experiencing his partner's unhappiness. Her distress may evoke anticipatory defensiveness in dealing with her unhappiness, which may have little to do with him. This then might lead to his withdrawal of empathy, intensifying his wife's unhappiness.

Because so many crucial adaptive patterns and protections are formed in childhood, individuals are limited by the level of intellectual and emotional understanding that they possess as children. Further, children's' developmental nature is to regard themselves as the center of their experience which could lead to a self-involved interpretation of events such as feeling that they are the cause or blame for occurrences. A frequent example of this situation occurs in situations of abuse and neglect, where the child feels responsible for the parent's behaviors. They are then locked into a pattern of anticipating abuse and trying desperately to figure out where they went wrong and what they can do to correct their deficiencies. This self-referential system also serves the adaptive function of giving the child some sense of control in feeling that there must be something s/he can do to repair and preserve the relationship with the parent. The acceptance of blame and guilt not only reinforces the sense of control, but also preserves a relationship, which would feel terrifying to be without. In accepting the blame, it is incomprehensible to a child to want to detach from an abusive parent, because if one's own parent is not caring, who else in the world would feel differently toward them?

In the activation of these projective or anticipatory systems of defense, couples lose sight of the fact that they might be in error as to their past interpretations, and they may significantly underestimate the fact that as adults, they have developed capabilities and assets which could help them to react to a situation differently, if they remained open to it, before initiating defensive maneuvers.

If past hurts have been prominent, then the activation of these anticipatory defenses is most often involuntary. This set of circumstances leads to a situation where the individual repeatedly experiences negative outcomes of his/her behavior and is puzzled as to how this comes about. Because the defensive maneuvers are not within his/her consciousness, the person is unaware how the defensiveness may contribute to, or bring about the very results that they are trying to avoid. A common example is of a shy and insecure young man who attributes a considerable amount of the insecurity to the fact that women do not respond to him, when the more complete picture is that he will attend a party and relate only minimally, if at all, to the women at the party. His fear of anticipated rejection almost automatically evokes behaviors, which cause him to remain on the periphery of activities, or to only have brief and awkward conversations with women he is introduced to.

Another significant difficulty with the anticipatory system of defense is the fact that partial similarities in the current situation are likely to trigger off stronger defensive reactions, which were geared to more comprehensive dangers in the past. For example, a wife might have some similar characteristics to a husband's rejecting or controlling mother causing an unconscious major distancing maneuver because the part-identification unconsciously triggered a more global defensive reaction to an unconsciously perceived mother figure.

Defense Mechanisms
As individuals experience many aspects of life, there are always potentially conflicting or opposites aspects of situations. While people need a degree of protection in their lives through predictability based on the projection of past experiences onto current situations, this process is also very responsible for holding onto negative and painful experiences which not only continue the pain, but also the reinforcement of negative notions about themselves, and their experience of the world as a dangerous or threatening environment. Protective mechanisms that are typically used by couples are denial, projection, externalization and devaluation, and detachment. These defense mechanisms are employed by individuals in a marriage in order to avoid anticipated hurt or rejection.

Denial
Chief among these defenses is denial, which allows persons not to attend to, and be actively aware of their behavior, expressions, or verbal communication, which reveals the truer underlying aspects of their thoughts and feelings. They will disavow evidence, which disputes their own consolidated view of themselves, fearing that any contradiction to their self-image will render them vulnerable to hurt, humiliation, or criticism. Denial allows for the addition of other mechanisms of defense such as projection, or externalization.

Projection

Projection is a fundamental process occurring out of a need for stability and protection, which involves the transfer of inner states of mind or qualities onto the environment. The recipient of the transfer may either be a partner, or the environment itself in the form of negative vibrations attached to a situation. Because repressed aspects of our life remain active and influential, even though they remain beyond every day awareness, projection is one mechanism to discharge the inner emotional tension that these unconscious aspects generate. In projection, the individual finds in others what s/he has been unable to accept in him/herself and can direct his/her energies to disparaging or criticizing others for these attributes. Other common means of discharging inner tension is through the pursuit of pleasure, sexuality, or mood altering substances such as drugs or alcohol.

Devaluation

Projection is often coupled with devaluation, which is the process of lowering the esteem or worth of the significant other by the projector, so as to avoid anticipated devaluation of oneself. By making the other less meaningful and valuable, any potential loss of that person is more easily borne, minimizing the risk of feeling loss, hurt, and rejection.

A detailed exploration of the varied defense mechanisms and their role in couple relationships is beyond the scope of this book. However, it is helpful to address their main attributes:

- **Defenses frequently make their appearance in a more intensified way when intimacy deepens with its concomitant threat of rejection or abandonment in those individuals with underlying and significant emotional insecurities.**
- **Defense mechanisms are necessary for normal adjustment but may become intensified leading to restricted and maladaptive behaviors and inner emotional suffering. Intensifications of defensive operations because of current precipitators may reactivate past vulnerabilities to the point where there is significant misinterpretation of present events.**

- Because defenses are replays of the past, (anticipation and prediction foster reenactment of past emotional experiences) there are unconscious, accompanying belief systems which are themselves repressed and not accessible to rational processes. The individual is usually convinced s/he is operating under adult, rational processes and these processes are what make him/her who they are. Direct challenges to these beliefs, behaviors, or attitudes are frequently met with frustration, anger, or a feeling of being criticized.

- These defenses create, for better or for worse, a stabilized sense of self which may be more or less realistic than the individual appreciates, which may be a significant problem in intimate relationships where there is significant discrepancy between the actual and idealized self.

- As the individual feels increasingly threatened, s/he tends to cling more to the defensive operations creating a vicious cycle of attack and defense with the partner. This conflict leads to a confusion of what the truer nature of the actual here and now problem between the couple actually is, as opposed to reactivation of pre-marital emotional problems.

- When defensive operations are more intensely mobilized, persons become hyper-focused on the current triggers of their sense of being threatened or hurt by their partner, and so, have a much diminished awareness that the hurt and threat they are currently experiencing derives from a more fundamental, and relevant set of past experiences. Indeed, the current interaction or trigger may only represent a smaller part of their underlying vulnerability with it's accompanying hurt and pain.

- Because defenses are ubiquitous in personality makeup, it is easy for each partner to cite the defenses of their partner as being responsible for the conflict, and avoid appreciating how each partner is contributing to the conflict.

There are many strategies for engaging and assisting couple conflict brought about in some measure by defensive operations triggered by the underlying emotional vulnerabilities of one or both of the partners. Given the aforementioned factors in defensive maneuver, it is helpful for the couple to come together in an atmosphere of patience, acceptance, and non-critical observation of what is transpiring at the individual and couple level. This exploration fosters a mutual search of themselves as individuals as well as a couple so as to reduce the fear of being real, and communicative of truer thoughts and feelings with reduced threat of criticism and rejection. When people come to understand that their misperceptions, maladaptive behaviors, and objectionable aspects of their personalities are understandable past attempts to cope and adapt, they are able to accept emotional correction more easily, and bring a compassion and empathy to the arena which is healing to both themselves and their partner. It makes more sense to couples when they can experience that they are reliving past hurts and vulnerabilities, and rather than being labeled as "crazy" or "unreasonable," they now understand how their past needs to protect themselves by accounting for what appears to be unreasonable behavior.

Marriages, which have a foundation of health, will be able to withstand these revelations of the truer nature of their partners and will grow from the experience of openness and realness in the relationship. It is the defensive operations that account for the problems more than the feelings themselves.

A frequent experience in couple's arguments is to have a surprised partner who has been just accused of various types of behavior answer with an unbelievable "but that's just the way you are!" The process of projection blinds couples to those qualities within themselves that they find objectionable. They are then less able to identify them and accept them as parts of themselves so as to bring meaningful help to themselves rather than to become condemnatory.

CASE HISTORY

> *After the breakup of his first marriage, Jack finally remet and married a woman he had known in his teenage years. He had idolized her as a youth and felt he would never be deserving enough to be loved by her. Following a whirlwind courtship in which some of his confidence was bolstered by alcohol, Jack became increasingly frightened that his wife would not think him manly enough. Over the ensuing years, he began to exhibit a belligerence and need for control, which undercut the joy of the initial years of the marriage. His sense of insecurity, which he dared not share with Louise less she think less of him, began to manifest itself sexually in terms of premature ejaculation. Louise was puzzled and dismayed at the turn their marriage was taking. She felt unattractive to Jack and felt he was losing his respect and love for her. In view of his controlling and dominating demeanor as well as his business success, she didn't understand his behavior as representing anxiety and insecurity. Jack's emotionally troubled background, in which he felt belittled and humiliated by his father and ignored by his mother, made him suspicious that he could be genuinely loved and respected.*

The above example is an instance in which one partner was experiencing significant anxieties stemming from inner feelings of insecurity and inadequacy which resulted from childhood experiences. These anxieties created a need to protect himself in the growing intimacy with his wife, who was fast becoming a potential threat. The history of this couple's difficulties is by no means uncommon in terms of a clear understanding and sharing of what their problems were. Louise had little notion of Jack's inner insecurities and Jack was unable to identify and admit his anxieties to Louise. Their arguments came to be focused on realistic but superficial issues, which engaged their attention to the point where both had little awareness of the more troubling aspects of their relationship. There are therapeutic techniques for assessing the role of early childhood issues in a couple's couple functioning.

Jack's significant childhood and adolescent emotional experiences sensitized him to the point where he maintained his defenses even in the face of Louise's appeals for mutual love and respect, and despite the fact that his behavior was jeopardizing the marriage. His fear of exposure and expected humiliation by her made him cling steadfastly to his perceptions of the situation in which he felt his wife was disrespectful of him and did not care for him the way she had when they were engaged.

For her part, Louise could not understand what happened to their initial loving relationship and felt that if he truly loved her, he would listen to her distress and change. In the face of the couple's continued problems, Louise was easily able to accept blame and responsibility for the problems in their marriage. This stemmed historically from her critical father who consistently berated her. In this way, she learned to perceive herself as less desirable and worthy as a person, and later as a wife. She had little understanding of her own unconscious processes or of the inner emotional anxieties, which Jack experienced. In their own unique way they colluded helping her to maintain a sense of stability and continuity with past definitions of herself and helping him to maintain his defensiveness.

Jack's personality problems reflect an over-preoccupation with the self, an overestimation of personal qualities, and unrealistic expectations of the self. This over evaluation is a compensation for underlying feelings of low self-esteem, and often, fears of abandonment. Problems similar to Jack's and Louise's type may not make their significant appearance until specific stresses or intimacy develops making it difficult for the intended partner to be prepared. If soft signs of emotional personality problems do make their appearance during courtship, the intended partner is likely to dismiss them as idiosyncratic, or behavior, which they believe, will change as their love deepens. The goal of therapy here involved a restructuring of both Jack's and Louise's internally based perceptions and expectations of each other. The primary goal was to deal with the aspects of each partner's personality that was specifically important to the couple relationship. This was accomplished through a sharing of each other's present and past experiences of pain and crises. First there was the use of "I" statements to convey feelings in the present, "I feel hurt when you …"; next these feelings were validated by the partner, "When I do …, you feel hurt."; and finally, these feelings were expressed in a historical context, "I used to feel these same kinds of feelings when …" In so doing, the couple became more empathic and supportive of each other. With Jack and Louise, this eventually led to a renewal of their original couple commitment to each other. During the therapeutic process, the couple learned about the role of their historically based unconscious processes on their couple relationship. In this way, they and their therapist were able to systemically diagnose, assess, and explore their couple relationship while also examining the linear links to the past.

41

RESOLVING CONFLICT

I'll be the judge, I'll be the jury, said cunning old Fury.
I'll try the whole case and condemn you to death.
(Lewis Carroll, Alice in Wonderland)

The Role of Insight

This brings up the whole question of what factors are linked with the successful resolution of couple conflict. And in all candor, it must be acknowledged that even though we can describe typical; processes of conflict, we know very little about the ways in which conflicts are limited or eliminated, or why some couples apparently do it better than others or why some couples do not do it at all.

One important factor, but which, unfortunately, operates in a very complex fashion, is the kind and amount of insight each partner develops into his or her own behavior and that of his or her partner. Some people appear totally incapable of comprehending underlying motivations for either their own or other's behavior while other people shrewdly anticipate one another and quickly recognize the long term consequences of given courses of action. This capacity for insight is not an all or none matter. Probably people can be ranged along a continuum according to how insightful they are. Differences among them are of degree rather than differences in kind.

In general, insight probably increases harmony in marriage. Many attacks, which couple partners make upon one another, are motivated out of hurt or fear. When one realizes that one's partner is only retaliating to protect him/herself from further injury or is afraid that s/he will be rejected, it becomes easier to react in ways that will lessen the hurt and fear rather than to leap to the attack itself. Once the process of understanding instead of hurting becomes established, the interaction takes on a spiral form. Here, we have the reverse of progressive conflict. An insightful, constructive response from one partner calls forth a constructive response from the other partner and so on. There may be critical points early in most marriages where the interaction takes on a spiral form. If it spirals negatively, estrangement soon results. If it spirals as a function of insight development, the areas of sharing may rapidly be enlarged.

This assumes of course that both partners show some insight development. In some cases undoubtedly they do. However, many couples are unequal in their capacities for insight, however, just as they are unequal in other regards. What happens when they are unequal in insight is less certain and leads to less optimistic conclusions.

If both partners are somewhat insightful, the more insightful partner is in a position to control the relationship. By anticipating more quickly and more accurately, s/he may be able to influence the partner. That power may be exercised either in the interests of both partners and the relationship or it may be used to profit the one partner at the expense of the other. Some exploitation of the less insightful partner may be frequent occurrence.

As stated, in some instances the partners' capacities for insight may differ markedly, leading to the domination of the more insightful partner by the less insightful one. Particularly if the less insightful partner is rigid to begin with, s/he may continue the conflict regardless of the ultimate harm done. The more insightful partner foreseeing the outcome may yield rather than destroy the relationship or the partner. There has been speculation on the quality of marriages in which the more insightful partner is dominated by the less insightful one. It stems from doubt that perceptive persons can endure continued domination and continue to invest themselves fully in the marriage. What appears plausible is that the insightful partner may gradually withdraw emotionally form the relationship. Outwardly the marriage may be quite stable, but emotionally it may be hollow.

However at least two studies failed to establish any relation between insight and couple adjustment. Corsini, studying 20 volunteer couples, concluded that there is no evidence that happiness in marriage is a function of understanding the mate. They found that the couples with the least togetherness could predict the responses of their partners as well as those who spent the most time together, and those married for only a short time could predict their partners' reactions as well as those who had been married for years.

EXERCISE: The Safe Environment

Creating a safe environment conducive to psychological growth is a major task to be accomplished during marriage. If you can accomplish this early, you are far ahead of the game. This safe environment is one in which both partners can co-exist, with full acceptance and love. In this way, they are each free to consider his/her position and approach, without fear of criticism from the other partner. The safe environment also affords each partner a safe place in which to re-explore the other, the relationship, and more importantly, him/herself. This is accomplished in the following way through the Couples Dialogue.

1. First the couple sits facing each other. They explore one issue. One speaks. S/he talks about his/her feelings around one issue. Keep focused. Do not bring up other issues from the past. Stay with the same issue. One partner verbalizes his/her feelings, using "I" statements. The other partner listens until the first partner is finished.

2. After the first partner is finished, the second partner repeats what the first partner has said. This called "mirroring." If the second partner leaves anything out or if s/he adds anything that is not wanted, the first partner corrects the second partner after s/he is finished.

3. The next step is for the first partner to explore the links to the past. So that s/he asks him/herself, when else in the past, when s/he was a little girl/boy did s/he also feel this way. Once again, the second partner listens.

4. After the first partner is finished, the second partner repeats and validates everything the first partner has said.

EXERCISE: The Couple's Dialogue

This exercise helps couples to learn to dialogue in a way that is conducive to intimacy and growth. It prevents arguments from escalating and facilitates understanding of the creation and maintenance of areas of sensitivity in relationships. This information is from Hendrix, Harville (1988). *Getting The Love That You Want.* New York:Henry Holt. It is recommended reading for any couple.

1. *Ask For An Appointment.* Appointment must be given as soon as possible.

2. *State Your Gripe Using "I "Statements.* Example. "I don't like it when you come home late."

3. *Partner Reflects Back Using Mirroring Technique.* "You don't like it when I come home late."

4. *State Your Gripe Moving To A Feeling Level.* "When you come home late, I feel like you don't care about me, like I'm not important to you. I feel unloved and sad."

5. *Partner Reflects Back Feeling.**** When I come home late, you feel like I don't care about you, like you're not important to me. You feel unloved and sad."

6. *Ask For Three Behavior Changes Around Your Gripe.* "I would like you to call if you're going to be late or not be late on Mondays and Wednesdays or not ever be late."

7. *Partner Grants One.* "I will call you if I'm going to be late."

8. *Say Thank You.*

***The individual can at this point go back in time when they felt the same way as a small child.

*5 a. **Rubber Banding Back.*** "If you were to stretch a rubber band back—back to when you were a little child, when you felt in a similar way, could you tell us what that was like."

The couple takes turns telling each other about how present issues are related to past experiences. In this way, each partner realizes s/he can be open, and able to share and express him/herself to the other. In this way, over time, the couple increases their intimacy and acceptance of each other.

EXERCISE: Communication Skills

Effective communication is based on mutual understanding and respect of each other's childhood experiences and how those struggles are manifested in the present relationship and personal struggles with that history. Couples can deal with their struggles by using the following communication techniques:

- Acknowledge that perceptions (the way we see things) are subjective— that no one is evil and that each person has his/her own point of view.

- Specific feelings rather than ideas associated with an issue should be expressed directly.

- The one who is doing the expressing of the feeling should include an acknowledgment of the positive side to the issue.

- Descriptions of thoughts, feelings, and perceptions of events should always be specific.

- Exactly what the expresser wants from the listener should be stated explicitly and specifically.

- The expresser should convey empathy for the listener's position. In this way, each can be a more effective helpmate and be experienced as that by the other.

EXERCISE: Change

Answer the following questions:

1. If you could change three things about your partner, what would
    you change?

    _____

    _____

    _____

2. If your partner could change three things about you, what three
    things do you think s/he would list?

    _____

    _____

    _____

3. What things really peeve you about your partner—what things
    really bother you about your partner?

    _____

    _____

    _____

4. If your partner were to list things that really peeve him/her about
    you, what do you think s/he would list? In other words, what
    things about you really bother your partner?

    _____

    _____

    _____

5. Does the image you have of your partner that you have now differ from that you had when you first got married? In what ways? Remember to list both negative and positive ways your partner's image has changed.

_____

_____

_____

6. What steps have you taken to resolve your problem? Explore these questions in your journal.

_____

_____

_____

7. What is the smallest amount of change that you would like to see in your relationship?

_____

_____

_____

8. What is the smallest amount of change that would constitute success for you? For your partner?

_____

_____

_____

9. How would you be different if you solved this particular problem?

_____

_____

_____

10. How would your partner be different if you solved this particular problem?

_____

_____

_____

11. How would your relationship be different if you solved this particular problem?

_____

_____

_____

EXERCISE: The Virginia Wolf Free For All

If couples feel a buildup of negative feelings toward the other, they could make an appointment with each other to have a Virginia Wolf free for all. Both partners must agree. At the appointed time, the one who requested the Free For All takes a bowl of water and places in the microwave for twenty minutes. For twenty minutes, s/he may yell, scream, curse and/or say whatever s/he wants to the other while the other stands or sits there, saying nothing. It is crucial that the other say nothing. When the bell goes off, the time is up, and the screaming must stop. Both parties say thank you to each other. The rules are that there will be no physical violence, nothing will get broken, nothing said during the Free For All will be brought up at a later time unless an appointment has been made in advance. The only rule is that **The Free For All Must End In Twenty Minutes.**

EXERCISE: Revisioning Your Relationship

The following are exercises that are designed to assist you in seeing that you can control your own destiny; that you are responsible for your own happiness; and that you can determine what kind of relationship you have.

Instant Replay

A method for seeing new possibilities in relationships is to take a gripe and do an instant replay. Often you will have an argument. Let's say you had this argument a few days ago. Each of you should take turns describing the argument as you each saw it in as much detail as you can. You should avoid interrupting each other. After each member has described the argument in great detail, then each of you could reenact the argument, but giving it a different ending. In this way you may see that things can be different—events do not always have to end in one way. You have control over the effects of your couple arguments. You can then "see" that there are other possibilities.

The Philosophy of "As If"

German Philosopher Vaihinger (66) presented the Philosophy of As If. This philosophy can be applied to your relationship. Basically, you can behave "as if." The situation presented is one, which provides a new possibility for you. For example, to a couple that said they were miserable, they can now "behave "as if" they were a happily married couple on Monday, Wednesday, and Friday. Tuesday, Thursday, and Saturday, behave the way they typically do—miserable. On Sunday, rest. This "as if" directive forces you to 1) image reality as a happily married couple and 2) behave as though you were that couple. Even if it is a temporary image, it is an image different than the one you typically hold. Further, behaving as if you were miserable often has the effect of the prescription "be spontaneous." Once it is verbalized, it is impossible to do. Couples often report that when they behaved as if they were miserable (their more typical behavior), they burst out laughing. Ultimately, the use of "as if" philosophy helps couples to conceptualize new meanings for their relationship, helps them to place the new meaning in an action context, and ultimately helps them understand that they have control over their life.

The Guessing Game

The guessing game also helps couples with a re-imaging of their partner. Over the course of the next week, do three nice things for your partner— things that your partner would like. However, do not tell your partner what the three things are. Each has to guess. The following week, the then tell each other what the nice things were and see if you guessed correctly. This exercise helps you first to place yourselves into your partner's shoes as you try to figure out what nice thing you could do for him or her. Next, it helps you to focus on the positive things that your partner does and in so doing helps you to notice that your partner does many more nice things than you originally thought. Many couples guess incorrectly and are surprised at how often their partner does positive things for them. This helps them to re-image each other.

The Appreciation Frame
"When the earth is fertile, the eggplants are large."
At the end of each day, tell each other what you appreciated about each other that day. Try to deepen this experience by asking each other, "Today, when did you feel that you appreciated me? What did I say or do that reminded you about how much you appreciated me? When did you feel that I appreciated you? How did you feel when I showed you that s/he cared, loved, etc. you?" This helps you to re-image each other and your relationship in a more positive frame.

The Future: New Possibilities
Future Focus enables you to visualize your relationship without problems. It stretches the rubber band into a future without problems and helps you visualize a more positive relationship. Questions like, "If you could stretch the rubber band three years into the future, what would your relationship look like? How would your relationship be different? How else would it be different?"

A **Miracle Question** can be used: "If a miracle were to happen tonight while you were asleep and tomorrow morning you awoke to find that you were happy in your relationship, what would be different? How would you know that this miracle had taken place? How could other people be able to tell without your telling them?"

The **Magic Wand** exercise is similar also. Here you can take turns holding a magic wand. Partner A asks, "If you could have three concrete specific wishes for behaviors from me that would make our relationship more positive, what would they be?" Then, the partner chooses one that s/he will grant. Then it is the partner B's turn.

These exercises, while they seem at first glance, simplistic, often have the complicated result of providing a context for change for the couple in that they provide the couple with seeds for a new reality — ones that hold a more positive image of the partner and the relationship.

A Ritual For A Fresh Start
Here, a ritual for a fresh start may be in order. At this time, couples can choose a date when they redo their marriage vows. They can do this alone or with their children, friends, relatives attending. Some couples prefer to rewrite their marriage vows, signifying the beginning of a new marriage. They often discuss the type of new marriage they want. Others rekindle positive feelings by restating their original vows. Along with redoing their commitment to each other and to the relationship, they can write down their future vision. This then becomes their future image, their future template for their relationship. Now, they have seen that they can write and rewrite their own future story.

42

IS MARRIAGE FOR A LIFETIME OBSOLETE?

You ask how long I'll love you, I'll tell you true
Until the twelfth of never, I'll still be loving you
I'll love you till the bluebells forget to bloom
I'll love you till the clover has lost its perfume
I'll love you till the poets run out of rhyme
Until the twelfth of never, and that's a long, long time
                                                    - Johnny Mathis

"Till death do us Part" has been an indisputable element of marriage vows in our society. The Western marriage has traditionally included the assumption of permanence, consistent with emphasis on marriage as providing security for the couple and their children and contributing to the stability of society as a whole. In recent years however, our values have undergone a major change. Couples believe in permanence as long as they meet each other's needs and their marriage is a happy one. But many now accept divorce as a solution to unhappy marriages. A widespread problem in contemporary marriages is that the partners do grow apart over time in interests, goals and values, until they have almost nothing left in common. While they may still like and respect each other, the companionship and romance may not have long since dwindled and died. This problem has led to some social scientists to suggest that people should engage in serial marriage. That is, if a couple grow apart and fail to meet each other's needs, they should divorce and find new partners who do.

Today, most people have probably accepted the idea of serial marriage, even though they realize that the price is living their marriage in the shadow of divorce. Of course, few people marry today with the clear expectation that their marriage will not be permanent. While they consider permanence desirable and hope to achieve it in their own marriage, they nevertheless consider it unrealistic. In fact, many have adopted the serial marriage orientation, believing in permanence only if they feel they have found the right person and consider themselves happy. Otherwise, they see divorce as an acceptable alternative. However, as marriage expert Jesse Bernard pointed out, there should be "no illusion that breaking up a marriage is any easier because it possibly was anticipated. there is always heartache in the breakdown of a human relationship as intense as that of marriage.

Nevertheless the majority of divorced persons will remarry and strive again to achieve their ideal, a happy and enduring marriage. And many who have not succeeded the first time will the second time. In short, permanence in marriage may be both difficult and idealistic in today's world, but it is not obsolete.

EXERCISES: Keeping Marriages Alive and Interesting

1. Date Night.
Choose one night a week when you date your partner. Take turns calling each other for a date. The one who calls plans the whole evening. On the appointed date night, the one who arranged the date gets dressed leaves the house only to return to pick up his/her date. The couple then goes out like they did when they were dating.

2. Guessing Game.
Each week choose three nice things that you can do for your partner. Remember these are things that you know your partner would enjoy. Do them but do not tell your partner what they are. Your partner must then guess what the three nice things were and tell you at the end of the week. Your partner is also doing three nice things for you and you must also try to guess what they are.

3. Care Days.
Both people participate in this activity. Each week, designate a care day. On this day, you will spend the day caring for and attending to each other in the same way that you did when you were dating each other.

4. Game Day.
Once a month, designate a day for game day. On this day, pick a silly activity that you both enjoy. It can be anything—the sillier the better. A mud fight, a whip cream fight. One couple went to a large mall, gave each other a half hour to hide in one of the stores. The task was that they then had to find each other. Playing hide and seek was fun for them because they had to focus on their partner—what s/he liked, where s/he would go.

5. Different Sex Day.
Once a month or whenever the couple decides, they partake in different sex day. This means that they do something different sexually. One couple had oriental night. After the children were in bed or, if the children are older, arrange for them to sleep overnight

at one of their friends, the couple dressed up and pretended that they were oriental. The husband donned his oriental outfit and the wife dressed up as a geisha. She greeted him at the door, pretending she was a geisha and they proceeded to have an oriental dinner, while listening to oriental music etc. This exercise can be as imaginative as the couple decides. The only requirements are that both members agree to the particular game and that the exercise they choose is different from what they usually do.

6. Fantasies.
In this game each partner chooses and writes out three of their favorite sexual fantasies. The written out fantasies are all placed in a bowl and the couple take turns choosing which fantasy they will play out on that evening. They will pretend that they are the people in the script and act out the roles. Both parties must agree. No physical harm is allowed.

EXERCISES: Sexuality Exploration Exercises

The Sensuous Feast

Make a list of foods that you consider to be sensuous. Tnen do what you want with the foods. You can eat them, lick them, or ....

Some foods you might want to consider are:

- chocolate anything
- ice cream
- cheese cake
- whipped cream
- French bread
- bananas
- avocados

EXERCISE: Exploring Your Feelings About Sex

Obligation or Pleasure ?

This exercise will help you learn how you feel about various sexual behaviors.

Working alone, using the scale from 1 to 5, with 1 indicating obligation and 5 indicating pleasure, respond to each activity.

	Obligation			Pleasure	
	1	2	3	4	5

Holding Hands
Kissing
French Kissing
Hugging
Hugging Naked
Breast/Nipple Touching
Masturbation (alone)
Masturbation (in Presence of partner)
Masturbating Each Other
Sexual Intercourse
Sleeping Together
Oral-Genital Sex (69)
Fellatio
Cunnilingus
Showering Together
Anal Stimulation
Anal Intercourse

Add other activities if you like.

Compare your answers with your partner. Some of your answers will be identical, or similar and others will differ. This exercise will help you see that understanding these similarities and differences are important in a relationship. When there are differences, how do you deal them? This exercise will open up discussion for sharing other pleasurable sexual activities.

Below list what you learned about yourself from exploring your sexuality.

_____

_____

_____

_____

_____

_____

_____

43 SOME CONCLUDING THOUGHTS

Throughout this book, I have tried to highlight and explore the various factors, which play a prominent role in the experience of loving and romantic feelings, the choice of a couple partner, and the types of interactions involved in couple relationships, which can affect the progress and outcome of the marriage. The statements, insights, and suggestions apply to all types of couple relationships, whether they be heterosexual, homosexual, bisexual, transgender, etc.

Marriage and parenthood, with its myriad demands, require the utmost attention and care if the family is to operate in the fuller dimension of intimacy and fulfillment. The processes of interaction derive from the various influences operating on each individual sociologically and psychologically. These processes act within and beyond the domain of conscious awareness, and are powerful determinants of the level of satisfaction and security that each family member feels.

While some form of bonding and family organization has been a part of world cultures for several thousands of years and appears to be the most natural culmination of moving into adulthood, the alarming degree of couple unhappiness, family conflict, and divorce makes it imperative that couples contemplating marriage have some idea of what they are entering into, and the steps they can reasonably take together and individually to ensure a more informed and optimistic decision. The benefits of working together and learning about an upcoming event can be seen in the Lamaze courses that many couples participate in when they make a decision to have natural childbirth. The joint effort and feeling of mutual involvement and support in the course helps to cement and enhance the sense of togetherness of the couple, and the meaningfulness of the event. It places an emotional priority on the activity of learning about the birth of a child.

When married people have had a chance in individual counseling or group therapy to review their decision to marry and their choice of mates, they often realize with amazement how little they knew of themselves or their mates at the time that important decision was made. It is often only with slow, patient, and insightful reconstruction that people begin to understand the role various sociological and psychological actors played in their life to bring them to where they are today.

As the human being is multidimensional and multipotentialed, so too are the needs and desires which move us toward marriage. These needs include; the social acceptance we experience when we live as a married couple; the diminished sense of aloneness and social isolation which marriage offers; the fulfillment of a desire to procreate which includes both the need for a sense of continuance after our death and the personal fulfillment of parenthood with it's joy of having and raising children; and the need to find emotional completeness in the union with a fellow human being.

The more mature the individual's capacity for loving, the greater will be his/her chances for actualizing these various needs in the relationship. The capacity to love plays a crucial role in an individual's sense of meaningfulness and fulfillment as well as being directly responsible for the degree of couple success. Why this is so has to do with what we feel is the essence of love: love, attunement, and connectedness.

In our evolution and revolution of scientific, spiritual, and psychological understanding, we have witnessed the increasing appreciation that all of life, both physical and biological processes, consists of an incredible interconnectedness and harmony that underlies the apparent discreet and isolated forms that register in our consciousness. Our well-being has come to be understood as connected to our attention to and appreciation of the fact that we live in a holistic and integrated environment, which we must respect. In the world of quantum effect, particularities of individual objects give way to an understanding of a wonderous interconnected and mutually interdependent whole. As our electronic sophistication in communications increases, as our economies become tied to the world market, as our technologies contribute to world pollution, we become more aware of our interdependence. Every action we take has a minute if not profound effect on our total environment and social milieu.

In the act of loving, care and attention is paid to one's relationship with the loved object. In a more mature type of love, the process of interaction and appreciation of the interconnectedness tends to transcend the needs and hence potential conflicts of the individual. In the appreciation of the other, there is an acceptance of the person as they are. This acceptance enhances appreciation, and this sense of appreciation of a person as they are, not as we wish or expect them to be, fosters the experience of love. This feeling of being accepted just as one is, is felt as being loved and is a powerful experience that releases us from fear and defensiveness. This feeling of loving and feeling loved is perceived as being directly meaningful. There is no further need to search or possess. The focused, attention and aware appreciation of what is, is itself experientially meaningful. This is the essential nature of loving. This powerful feeling transcends the satisfaction we get from accomplishment, pride and possession. This can be experienced for oneself, and need not be thought of as a philosophical or hypothetical concept. While we tend to think of the intense period of romantic infatuation as temporary and superficial, it actually demonstrates the capacity within us to experience a deeper and more enduring type of love. In the period of romantic ecstasy, we are in our most open and participatory self. All too soon, our protective mechanisms tiptoe in to begin to shut us down and bring us back to what we consider our usual "normal" state of mind. While this state of heightened excitement we call romantic love is indeed transitory for most of us, it does nevertheless speak to us of the power of surrender, of letting go, of intensely feeling genuinely loved and loving.

EXERCISE: To My Partner, My Most Important Person

This exercise involves writing a letter to your partner, the most important person in your life. Think about writing this letter as coming directly from your heart, holding nothing back. Before writing the letter, make a list of memories, images, words, and feelings that you have about your partner. When making this list, don't think about the words, just let them spill out of your consciousness. The list contains words reminding you of close times in the relationship and times of difficulty or separation. It contains memories that will help you understand the major stages of the relationship. The list is only words, words that come to you as you think about this most important person.

___	___	___
___	___	___
___	___	___
___	___	___
___	___	___
___	___	___
___	___	___
___	___	___
___	___	___
___	___	___
___	___	___

When you are finished with your list, look it over and if it isn't complete, add more words. There will words on the list that you haven't thought about in along time. Now go down the list and circle the items you want to write most about in your letter. Now begin to write the letter. This letter will help you see your relationship more clearly than you ever have before.

Dear_____,

_____

_____

_____

_____

_____

_____

_____

_____

_____

_____

_____

_____

_____

_____

_____

_____

_____

_____

For everything there is a season, and a time to every purpose under heaven:
a time to be born and a time to die;
a time to plant, and a time to pluck up what is planted;
a time to kill, and a time to heal;
a time to break down, and a time to build up;
a time to weep, and a time to laugh;
a time to mourn, and a time to dance;
a time to cast away stones, and a time to gather stones together;
a time to embrace, and a time to refrain from embracing;
a time to seek, and a time to lose;
a time to keep, and a time to cast away;
a time to rend, and time to sew;
a time to keep silent, and a time to speak;
a time to love, and a time to hate;
a time for war, and a time for peace. (Ecclesiastes 3: 1-8)

I see trees of green, red roses too
I see them bloom for me and you
And I think to myself
What a wonderful world
I see skies of blue
And clouds of white
The bright, blessed day
The dark, sacred night
And I think to myself
What a wonderful world
The colors of the rainbow, so pretty in the sky
Are also faces of the people going by
I see friends shaking hands, saying how do you do
They're really saying, I love you
I hear babies cry, I watch them grow
They'll learn much more than I'll ever know
And I think to myself
What a wonderful world. (Louis Armstrong)

Printed in the United States
By Bookmasters